P9-DXR-474

KAMIKAZE

KAMIKAZE

DAVID BROWN

GALLERY BOOKS
An imprint of W.H. Smith Publishers Inc.
112 Madison Avenue
New York, New York 10016

Published by Gallery Books
A Division of W.H. Smith Publishers Inc.
112 Madison Avenue
New York, New York 10016

Produced by
Brompton Books Corp.
15 Sherwood Place
Greenwich, CT 06830

ISBN 0-8317-2671-7

Printed in Hong Kong

10 9 8 7 6 5 4 3 2 1

CONTENTS

PAGE 1: 11 April 1945: even at full depression, the *Missouri*'s AA guns will not bear on the 'Zero' driving in to bounce off the battleship's side and into the sea.

PAGE 2 (INSET): 4 May 1945: *Sangamon*'s flight deck was bowed upwards and both elevators blown out by the explosion of a bomb carried through the flight deck by the *kamikaze.*

PAGE 2 (MAIN PICTURE): 11 May 1945: the first *kamikaze* to hit the *Bunker Hill* started fires in the after deck park, destroying or severely damaging a score of Grumman Avengers and Curtiss Helldivers.

LEFT: 21 February 1945: the *Saratoga*'s fire-fighting teams bring under control the fierce blaze caused by the third 'Zero' to hit the ship.

AT 1100 hours local time on 19 June 1944, an unknown Japanese Navy pilot deliberately crashed his burning Mitsubishi 'Zero-Sen' fighter-bomber into the side of the US battleship *Indiana*, to the northwest of Guam, Mariana Islands. It was by no means the first suicide attack by a doomed aircraft and it merely dented its armored target, but it almost certainly provided the germ of an idea which, when it flowered, was to introduce a new and horrible dimension to what was already a naval war of unprecedented ferocity.

The war in the Pacific was now 30 months old. The first six months had seen the US and Allied navies sustain terrible losses as the Japanese pushed out the boundaries of their conquests and occupations as far as they were to go. The next nine-month phase began with two carrier battles, which

The move to an advanced base did not improve readiness and the aircrew were thoroughly out of practice on the eve of the Battle of the Philippine Sea, a month later.

On 19 June 1944 the third wartime generation of Japanese carrier aviators was virtually wiped out. Of 373 aircraft flown off to attack the US Fifth Fleet, 261 failed to return. Thirty of those which did return were badly damaged, another 22 aircraft and many aircrew were lost in two large carriers sunk by US Navy submarines, and over 50 land-based aircraft were shot down. Some 500 trained Japanese Naval Air Force (JNAF) aircrew had been expended in exchange for minor damage to two aircraft carriers and two battleships, and the loss of 30 American carrier aircraft and just 27 pilots and crewmen.

The main blow of Operation A-Go had

CHAPTER 1

THE FIRST
KAMIKAZES

cost the Japanese Navy fully half of the experienced carrier aircrew who had spearheaded the outward drive, and continued with the attrition of the Guadalcanal campaign, which accounted for most of the rest. During 1943, the Japanese Navy attempted to build up new carrier air groups while the carriers were being repaired, but frittered away men and aircraft by sending them to bolster the land-based units in the Southwest Pacific, where US forces were leapfrogging up the Solomon Islands chain toward the vital Japanese bastion at Rabaul.

The Japanese carrier fleet was thus in no condition to oppose the US Navy's Central Pacific offensive, which began in earnest in November 1943 with the invasion of the Gilbert Islands. Even by mid-May 1944, when the fleet left its training bases to concentrate in anticipation of the next American move, only two of the three carrier squadrons could claim to have more than a nucleus of adequately trained air groups.

been, by any standard, a disaster for the Imperial Japanese Navy. But, despite the seemingly awesome efficiency of the US Navy's experienced fighter squadrons and their controllers, veterans of eight major operations in as many months, a major success had nearly been achieved. Over 50 Japanese aircraft broke through, piecemeal or in small disciplined formations, to miss a dozen ships, including five out of the seven large fast carriers, by the narrowest of margins. Translated into bomb and torpedo hits, this penetration of the best air defense system then in existence would have turned defeat into a major tactical victory, the fruits of which would have included precious time for the Japanese Empire.

But for all their courage and determination, this generation of Japanese carrier aircrew lacked the experience and skill of their 1941-42 predecessors and their failure to brake the accelerating US Pacific offensive meant that there would never be time for

LEFT: 20 June 1944: Avengers and Helldivers of *Yorktown*'s Air Group 1 outbound for the counter-strike on the Japanese Mobile Fleet, to the west of the Marianas.

their successors to acquire these attributes.

The scale of the defeat in the Philippine Sea was fully appreciated by the Japanese commanders. This went far beyond acceptance that the loss of the Marianas – Saipan, Tinian and Guam – was inevitable: even the war could be lost. For the first time, some admirals even began to talk of seeking peace. In the meantime, they had to evolve a strategy, devise tactics and provide resources to counter the next US move toward the heart of the Japanese Empire.

The strategy was decided for them by geography and their own reduced circumstances. Four contingency plans (Sho-Go 1-4) were drawn up to cover all the possibilities, but the Philippine Islands were the obvious target for the next invasion. Dominating the southwestern sea approaches, and therefore the route between Japan and the empire's main sources of tin, rubber and, above all, oil, the islands held the key to economic as well as military survival. The Philippines were emotionally important to the United States, whose forces had been comprehensively defeated there in the opening months of the war in the US Army's counterpart to Pearl Harbor, but more crucial was their military value, with good fleet anchorages, established airfields and space and facilities to support the army, within 1500 miles (2400 kilometers) of Tokyo. To defend the islands, the Imperial Japanese Army concentrated the bulk of its garrison on Luzon and trained mobile detachments to counterattack American beachheads on the other islands. The army and navy deployed large numbers of aircraft as an air garrison, which would be the first into action against the invaders, but the decisive force would have to be naval, with the full remaining strength of the fleet intervening to destroy the amphibious shipping and drive off the supporting warships.

The Japanese carriers were not expected to play their accustomed leading role in this strategy. Although the planners had assumed that the American blow would not fall before mid-November 1944, by when three new carriers would have more than made up for the June 1944 losses, there was little prospect that there would be sufficient trained pilots to man them. There was no shortage of suitable personnel, for the training 'pipeline' was full of enthusiastic young men with proven aptitude and whose technical education was often far superior to that of their American opposite numbers.

RIGHT: May 1945: a burning Yokosuka 'Frances' misses astern of one of TG 52.1's escort carriers off Okinawa.

BELOW RIGHT: 17 June 1944: overture to the 'Turkey Shoot' – land-based aircraft delivered the first major air attack on US carriers off Saipan; only the *Fanshaw Bay* was hit and few of the 50 Japanese aircraft returned to Yap.

BELOW: 19 June 1944: noon: three torpedo-bombers break through the CAP and are shot down by the AA gunfire of Task Group 58.3; the light carrier *Princeton*, right, was narrowly missed by their torpedoes.

The most serious problem for the JNAF was that of fuel shortage which became acute after the summer of 1944, due primarily to the US submarines' successes against tanker traffic. The lack of fuel affected operational flight and carrier training, for the ships' sea-time was severely rationed to provide a reserve of oil for actual operations, in which their effectiveness would be limited in consequence of their air groups' lack of practice.

The credit for conceiving tactics which were intended to enable attack aircraft to penetrate US Navy defenses and to compensate for the inadequacy of the Japanese naval pilots' training has been given to Captain Eiichiro Jyo, who had commanded the light carrier *Chiyoda* in the Battle of the Philippine Sea. Half of the aircraft embarked in the three ships of Carrier Division Three, to which the *Chiyoda* belonged, were obsolescent 'Zero 21' fighters each modified to carry a 550lb bomb. Faster than the fixed-landing gear Aichi 'Val' dive-bombers which had caused so much damage during the first year of the war and easier to fly than the new Yokosuka 'Judy,' the fighter-bombers were allocated to the newly-formed 333rd Air Group, which was known

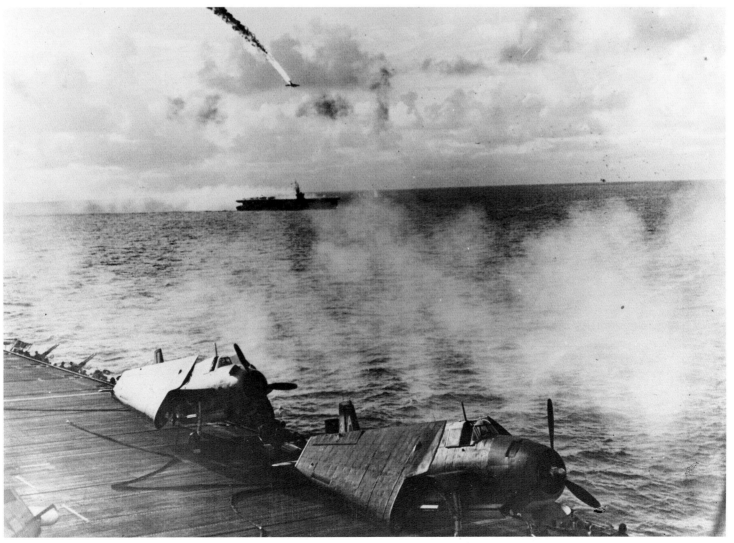

LEFT: The Mitsubishi A6M 'Zero', designed as an interceptor but outmoded by 1944, became the main weapon of the Imperial Japanese Navy's *Kamikaze* Corps.

RIGHT: Photographs of Japanese Army Air Force suicide aircraft are rare – Usaburo Ihara's painting depicts Nakajima 'Oscar' fighter-bombers of the 89th Suicide Unit.

BELOW: The Yokosuka 'Judy' dive-bomber was in many ways the ideal suicide aircraft.

as the 'Special Attack Unit' ('*Tokebetsu Kogeki Kai*'), dedicated to attacks on US carriers. In the event, on 19 June 1944 the 43 fighter-bombers attacked the American battleship task group and about a dozen got through – of these one scored a direct hit on the *South Dakota* and two made suicide attacks, one of which actually hit the *Indiana*.

Deeply impressed by American efficiency and the apparent success of Japanese self-lessness, Jyo forwarded to the commander of the Japanese carrier forces (the Mobile Fleet), Vice-Admiral Tokusaburo Ozawa, his recommendation that conventional air attacks on shipping should be supplemented by 'the organization of special attack units to carry out crash-dive tactics'. Rear Admiral Sueo Obayashi, who commanded CarDiv Three, supported Jyo but Ozawa did not and nor did his superior, Admiral Soemu Toyoda, the Commander-in-Chief, Combined Fleet. Like others in the higher echelons of the Imperial Japanese Navy, these senior officers continued to believe that the many good, and as yet un-tried, land-based attack units and the sur-viving carrier veterans could achieve deci-sive results with the new fighter and attack aircraft coming into naval service – 'the time was not yet ripe, it was too early to use it.'

This was not the opinion of Rear Admiral Takajiro Ohnishi, head of the naval aviation division of the Ministry of Munitions and de-signated to take command in October 1944 of the First Air Fleet, land-based in the northern Philippines. In his support of suicide attacks as an addition to the Japanese Navy's repertoire, Ohnishi and his followers were influenced by mysticism as much as by the predicted practical benefits. The quasi-religious cult of *Bushido*, a philo-sophy which taught absolute loyalty, obedi-ence and indebtedness to superiors, had originated in the thirteenth century as a moral code for the warrior classes, the *sam-urai*, a closed caste. When the *samurai* were legally abolished in 1871 their 'private' code was absorbed into the *Shinto* cult and adopted by the nation as a whole, with the public education system teaching that the loyalty and self-sacrifice of all were now due to the emperor, the divine head of a secular belief.

Shinto came readily to the hand of the militarists and ultra-nationalists who domi-nated Japanese politics after World War I and who found ready adherents in junior and middle-ranking army and naval officers. The *samurai* had accepted death in the ser-vice of their overlords with stoicism – their heirs glorified death in battle as a sacrifice

LEFT: The 'father' of the Japanese Navy's *Kamikaze* Corps, Rear Admiral Takajiro Ohnishi, who took command of the First Air Fleet in the Philippines shortly after the American landings on Leyte.

RIGHT: Admiral Soemu Toyoda, the CinC Combined Fleet, who initially opposed suicide tactics but had to acknowledge that they alone were able to inflict substantial damage on the Allied Navies.

for the emperor which earned the victim posthumous promotion. A thousand years after the Norse berserkers began to abandon hopes of the everlasting banquet which awaited them in Valhalla, the Japanese re-dedicated the Yasukuni Shrine, near the Imperial Palace in Tokyo, as the spiritual home of those who had died for Japan and where they would 'consort in eternal fellowship'.

In August 1944, a suggestion by a JNAF transport pilot, Ensign Ohta, that a manned glider-bomb, carried to within reach of its target by a mother-plane, should be developed for attacks on shipping, was taken up officially. The design was worked out by the Aeronautical Research Department of Tokyo University and the Yokosuka Naval Air Arsenal was given the task of building and testing prototypes. In his position in the highly centralized naval aviation supply organization, Rear Admiral Ohnishi cannot have been ignorant of the project and, in the light of his subsequent career, must be suspected of being its patron. And although the C-in-C, Combined Fleet, had not sanctioned the preparation of suicide units, at the end of September 1944 the 721st Air

Group was formed at Konoike, near Yokosuka, to develop tactics and training methods for the glider-bomb, which was named 'Ohka' (Cherry Blossom). Unusually for late 1944, this unit was not administered by one of the JNAF's air fleets but by the Yokosuka Naval District, which was answerable not to Combined Fleet but to the Imperial General Headquarters, to which Ohnishi owed eventual allegiance. As there can be no question that the headquarters had any hand in the introduction of deliberate suicide tactics, Ohnishi and his supporters, convinced by their own self-righteous code, must also be suspected of flouting their superiors in Combined Fleet and Imperial HQ, and, thereby, the emperor himself.

The US Navy moved more quickly than the Japanese planners had expected. The next amphibious thrust after the Marianas came not at the Philippines but against the Palau Islands, to the east of Mindanao, in mid-September 1944. No naval or air resistance was encountered by the assault forces, but the fast carrier groups supporting the invasion took the war to the enemy

RIGHT: Admiral William F Halsey, Commander, US Third Fleet: his handling of the fleet during the Philippines campaigns resulted in criticism at the time, but his determined aggressiveness was never questioned.

BELOW RIGHT: Ensign Ohta's 'Ohka' was conceived as a rocket-boosted manned glider-bomb. An attempt to extend its range by the replacement of the rockets by a small jet engine was a failure, due to its low power.

BELOW: The commander of a *kamikaze* unit, an Imperial Japanese Navy lieutenant, receives his orders.

and struck at airfields and shipping throughout the Philippines. No strikes were attempted against the American carriers, which were credited with the destruction of nearly 900 Japanese Army and JNAF aircraft (mostly on the ground) during this one-sided 17-day offensive. Although the true figure was probably much lower, the losses were nonetheless devastating and not readily replaced. When Ohnishi, promoted to vice-admiral, assumed command of the First Air Fleet on 17 October 1944, he had no more than 200 effective aircraft.

The lack of a Japanese response to these operations led Admiral William Halsey, commanding Task Force 38, the Fast Carrier Task Force, to recommend that the intended schedule for step-by-step amphibious progress should be cancelled and that the next target should be Leyte Island. Leyte, whose attractions included a broad coastal plain suitable for the construction of airfields and excellent anchorages for an entire fleet, was to have been invaded on 20 December according to the original timetable, but 'A-Day' was brought forward by two months to 20 October.

THE US Fast Carrier Task Force began precursor operations for the Leyte operation on 10 October 1944. Nine large and eight 'light' carriers, with over 1000 aircraft embarked, attacked Okinawa, northern Luzon and Formosa over the period of a week to disrupt the forces, particularly air forces, which could support or reinforce the Philippine garrisons. The first massive strike, on Okinawa on 10 December, prompted the Combined Fleet to order Sho-Go 2 to be put into effect to counter the threat of invasion in the Formosa-Okinawa-Kyushu area.

One of the first moves thereafter was to order Admiral Ozawa to despatch his more experienced aircrew to reinforce Second Air Fleet which had been caught in the midst of a move from Kyushu to Formosa. Ozawa attempted to seek a reprieve for his half-trained carrier air groups, but Admiral

succeeded only in clipping the deck-edges of the *Franklin* and her sister-ship, the *Hancock*, both of which sustained minor damage from bombs which exploded in the water alongside. Even had these incidents led to the loss of a ship, the Fast Carrier Task Force could have continued to support the Leyte invasion. The Japanese, on the other hand, could not afford the loss of nearly 500 aircraft (300 naval, 200 army) on the eve of this crucial campaign.

One loss was entirely unnecessary. On 15 October, First Air Fleet found a carrier task group within range and during the afternoon Rear Admiral Masafumi Arima, commander of the 26th Air Flotilla, personally led a heavily-escorted strike, making it obvious before he left that he intended to deliver a suicide attack. Although the staff of First Air Fleet claimed that the admiral

CHAPTER 2

THE BATTLE FOR LEYTE

Toyoda insisted and 172 aircraft were transferred for land-based operations. They became caught up in one of the most violent sea-air battles of the war, with the US carrier fleet standing its ground for four days (13-16 October) against the heaviest strikes that the JNAF and JAAF could mount from Kyushu and Formosa. The Japanese pilots who returned believed that they had hit and at least badly damaged 10 aircraft carriers. The staffs of Second Air Fleet and Combined Fleet discounted all but four of these claims – a prudent reduction which was still over-optimistic.

The reality was that two US cruisers had been severely damaged by torpedoes (one twice), the carrier *Franklin* was superficially damaged by a twin-engined Mitsubishi 'Betty' which failed to avoid her after an unsuccessful dusk torpedo drop, and the same happened to the antiaircraft cruiser *Reno* on the following evening. The level and dive-bombers had even less success, for they

had dived into a carrier, he failed to get near a ship, for Task Group 38.4's Combat Air Patrols (CAP) broke up the raid, destroying a score of aircraft, including Arima's, at long range. Whatever may have been the moral value to the pro-suicide fanatics in their recruitment of volunteers of this action, the loss of an experienced and able commander on the eve of the decisive battle was ill-timed.

On 17 October 1944, as the US carriers withdrew to the east, Admiral Toyoda, appreciating that there was little immediate threat of landings on Formosa and the islands to the north, alerted all his forces for the defense of the Philippines. By the next day, following the seizure of islands in the approaches to Leyte Gulf by US Rangers and as the result of intercepted voice radio traffic which confirmed Leyte as the target, Sho-Go 1 was ordered and the greater part of the surviving Japanese fleet sailed from its bases: the main battle fleet from Singapore,

LEFT: Mabalacat, October 1944: Rear Admiral Ohnishi pours the ceremonial cup of sake for those about to die.

a smaller battleship and cruiser squadron from the Formosa area, and four carriers from the Inland Sea of Japan. The battleships and cruisers were to be the main striking force, to attack the amphibious shipping and the close covering groups; Ozawa's carriers, with only 116 aircraft between them, were to draw off the US fast carriers which they could scarcely be expected to fight.

Vice-Admiral Ohnishi arrived in Manila to take command of First Air Fleet on 17 October. His three combat air groups could together muster barely 70 serviceable fighters and attack aircraft and 30 reconnaissance and night-fighters. Only in his pilots was he fortunate, for many of them were veterans by late 1944 standards, with an average of over 300 flying hours since joining their units. On 19 October, the admiral visited the fighter unit (201st Air Group) at Mabalacat and, supported by his staff, expounded his view that only suicide attack provided an effective means of striking at the US Navy's carriers. The acting air group commander took counsel of his officers and agreed to organize a 'special attack unit' within the 201st Air Group. He then assembled his petty officer pilots and called for volunteers – all 23 did so; the surviving eyewitness who reported the scene failed to add that the inducement of double promotion – two ranks instead of the customary one – awaited those who deliberately crashed into a carrier. An inexperienced but enthusiastic young officer

was then selected to volunteer to command the 'Shimpu Attack Unit,' which was officially formed on 20 October with an establishment of 26 Mitsubishi 'Zero 32' (or 'Hamp,' as it was known to Allied pilots) fighter-bombers. His orders were to be ready to commence operations by 25 October. The naval kamikaze or 'Special Attack Corps' had been born, an inappropriate expression when all its flying personnel had chosen death from the moment of volunteering.

The main source for the account of naval kamikaze operations, Captain Rikibei Inoguchi, Ohnishi's chief of staff, flatly denied that the JAAF took part in the initial attacks, but there is good evidence to suggest that the Japanese Fourth Air Army in the Philippines quickly followed the lead of the 1st Air Flotilla and even carried out the first suicide attack of the campaign. It is known that they certainly delivered later attacks. Regrettably, no accounts of such activity have survived, but it would appear that the JAAF suicide units were tasked with attacks on transports off the beaches in support of conventional bombers which were known to have been ordered to attack troops ashore. The army pilots, both those who had survived the September carrier attacks and their replacements drawn from China and the Home Islands, were very experienced by 1944 Japanese standards and the fighter squadrons were armed in part with the newest aircraft.

The US Army began the main landing on

BELOW: 20 October 1944: 'H'-Hour at Leyte – LCAs head for the beaches, with LSTs awaiting their turn; the assault transports are anchored at top left, while a fast transport (APD) is crossing from right to left in the center of the photograph.

Leyte on 20 October 1944. Husbanding their resources for use in support of the naval forces, the Japanese air forces were remarkably quiet and it was not until late afternoon that the only attack of the day by First Air Fleet approached and succeeded in torpedoing a US Navy cruiser. At dawn the next day, a JAAF fighter-bomber appoached undetected and delivered a completely successful crash-diving attack on the cruiser HMAS *Australia*. Aiming for the bridge, the pilot actually flew into the substantial foremast, after striking the gunnery director control tower. A gasoline fire enveloped the superstructure, killing the ship's commanding officer and 21 men. Fifty-five others were injured and the ship had to withdraw for essential repairs.

Bad weather from 21 to 23 October prevented further raids on the amphibious area but covered the arrival of 300 aircraft of Vice-Admiral Shigeru Fukudome's Second Air Fleet from Formosa. With the JAAF bombers, the new arrivals attacked shipping in Leyte Gulf throughout 24 October and, although they lost heavily to the fighters from the escort carriers protecting the invasion force, they damaged three ships. During the morning, a JAAF bomber, attempting to crash into an assault transport, overshot and hit a 1100-ton US Navy fleet tug. The USS *Sonoma* caught fire and was abandoned. Attempts to beach her on Dio Island were unsuccessful and late in the afternoon she foundered at anchor – the first ship actually to be lost to 'tai-atari' (literally, 'bodily-crashing').

The significance of these deliberate attacks was for the time being lost upon the US Navy, for Second Air Fleet inflicted a more serious loss on the 24th. As the two groups of US fast carriers 'on the line' off Leyte moved up to strike at the main Japanese battle fleet early in the forenoon, they came under heavy air attack. The Grumman Hellcat fighters broke up three waves, each of about 50 aircraft, but a Yokosuka 'Judy' of the 141st Air Group got through under the low cloud, hit the light carrier *Princeton* and escaped. The *Princeton* burned for eight hours, while the undamaged carriers launched wave after wave of strikes against the Japanese main fleet, sinking the battleship *Musashi* and one destroyer. In the end, the American carrier had to be scuttled, the first US fast carrier to be lost for two years.

Admiral Ozawa's diversionary carrier force played no direct part in this loss. Thirty-six attack aircraft, two shadowers and an escort of 40 fighters – the last Japanese carrier aircraft mission – flew off to strike at the *Princeton*'s task group. It was intended to be a one-way trip, not because the pilots were *kamikazes*, but because they were too inexperienced to find and land back on board their own ships and had been ordered to land ashore on Luzon. Six 'Judies' got past the CAPs but missed the American carriers. Fewer than 30 aircraft of all types arrived on Philippine airfields – they did not even compensate for Second Air Fleet's losses on this day but they were added to the reserve available for suicide attacks and the pilots joined the ranks of Ohnishi's volunteers.

25 October was the critical day of Sho-Go. While Ozawa's carriers attempted to attract the attention of the Fast Carrier Task Force, the main battle fleet broke out into the open waters of the Pacific to the north of Leyte, aiming to pass around Samar Island and take the US amphibious fleet from the north, while a smaller, but still powerful squadron passed to the south of Leyte, through the Surigao Straits. Ohnishi's first *kamikazes* were standing by to play their part, keyed up to attack the American carriers as soon as they could be located. To achieve any great measure of success, the blows had to coincide, at about dawn, but already the battle fleet had been badly delayed by the US carrier air attacks on the 24th.

The southern force stuck to its timetable, attempted to force the Surigao Straits without any support and was virtually destroyed by the undistracted destroyers and battleships from the Allied support groups in Leyte Gulf. Ozawa succeeded in drawing off the US fast carriers, whose commander, Halsey, lost sight of his broader responsibilities in his obsession with sinking Japanese carriers, and the Japanese main force slipped through. By mischance, the battleships and heavy cruisers ran into one of the three US escort carrier units to the east of Samar, half an hour after sunrise on the 25th. The Battle of Samar was fought between about 0700 and 0930: the Japanese heavy ships failed to come properly to grips with the six small, slow carriers of Task Unit 77.4.3 and their seven escorts, despite over 10 knots' speed advantage and heavy guns which far outranged the Americans' five-inch weapons. Although only one carrier was sunk, four others suffered varying degrees of damage and three of their escorts were sunk.

As this epic struggle was approaching a critical stage for the carriers, the first JNAF *kamikazes* struck. Had they gone for the escort carrier unit which was then beginning to come under accurate gunfire, their intervention might have been dramatically decisive, but the 201st Air Group was not cooperating directly with the Japanese

ABOVE: 24 October 1944: the battleship *Musashi* is hit by bombs and torpedoes in the Sibuyan Sea as the aircraft of TF 38 try to stop the Japanese Center Force.

ABOVE RIGHT: 25 October 1944: 0800 – *Suwanee* is hit for the first time but two hours later is able to operate aircraft.

LEFT: 25 October 1944: the Battle of Samar – *Gambier Bay*, straggling behind Taffy Three and seen framed by the smoke-screen laid by one of her sister-ships, is straddled by a Japanese shell salvo.

ABOVE: October 1944: carrying a 550-pound bomb, a 'Zero' taxies out for a suicide mission against the US fleet off the Philippines; the landing gear and bomb of a second 'Zero' can be seen behind.

battle fleet, it was searching for targets of opportunity. After a reconnaissance of Leyte Gulf, five 'special attack' 'Zeroes' and three escorting fighters headed out to the open ocean and, some 40 miles southwest of the area of the battle, came across another six escort carriers (Task Unit 77.4.1), which had just launched a strike against the Japanese fleet. Distracted by the confusion of the air-surface operation and by their own

aircraft, the US ships failed to detect the approach of the Japanese force and there was only short warning before, at 0740, the *Santee* was struck by an aircraft on the port side of her flight deck. Within a minute, the *Petrof Bay* was near-missed by a second *kamikaze* and the *Sangamon* was struck a glancing blow by a bomb dropped by an aircraft which crashed well wide. The bomb exploded in the air but inflicted only superficial damage.

The *Santee*'s fires, started by the explosion of the 'Zero's' bomb in the hangar, were under control within 11 minutes, but 16 men lost their lives. Four minutes later she was shaken by a heavy underwater explosion, which caused flooding and a five-degree list, but no additional casualties. Even after she had been inspected in dock, it was considered that this damage was probably due to the explosion of one of the damaged depth-charges which were being jettisoned from the hangar by the firefighters, and it was not until after the war that it was realized that the *Santee* had been torpedoed by the Japanese submarine *I.56*.

At 0800, a lone 'Zero' evaded the same unit's small CAP and got through the antiaircraft barrage to score the perfect hit, on the center-line of the *Suwanee*'s flight deck,

between the aircraft elevators. The engine and bomb went through the wooden flight deck, leaving a 10-foot diameter hole, and the bomb then exploded, blowing a 25-foot hole in the hangar deck and starting a minor fire. Casualties were quite heavy, but the damaged flight deck was quickly patched and two hours later the ship was once again able to land her aircraft. The four un-damaged carriers of TU 77.4.1 continued to strike at the Japanese fleet.

The battleships and surviving cruisers, badly mauled by the carriers' aircraft, hauled off shortly before 0930. The crisis of the Battle of Leyte Gulf was over – the deci-sive victories had been won, not by the fast carriers, which were pursuing a symbolic but empty success in the north, sinking all four of Ozawa's aircraft-less carriers (Jyo, the original sponsor of suicide attack, died with his ship, the *Chiyoda*), but by the old battleships and destroyers in the south and the escort carrier aviators in the center, off Samar. Now was indeed the time for desper-ate measures and to this extent Ohnishi's fanaticism can be justified as foresight, for

he had conditioned a major proportion of the JNAF's frontline aviators to the idea of self-immolation in the *Bushido* spirit. However, volunteer *kamikazes* and spur-of-the-moment suiciders were indistinguishable to their victims.

Task Unit 77.4.3's position was now known to the land-based air fleets and at least two attack missions took off before the end of the battle, but too late to intervene. First to arrive was another dedicated *kami-kaze* strike. At 1050 five 'Zeroes' got past the Grumman Wildcat fighters of the CAP and dived at the carriers. One missed, another strafed the destroyer escort *Richard M Rowell* which shot it down well wide, a third exploded in the wake of the *White Plains*, riddling her stern with bomb fragments and adding to the underwater damage previous-ly suffered from numerous shell near-mis-ses. The next clipped the edge of the *Kitkun Bay*'s flight deck and hit the sea 25 yards off her bow, where the bomb exploded. Only slightly damaged by shell near-misses in the earlier action, the carrier escaped with minor damage caused by splinters and

ABOVE: 25 October 1944: 1050 – *White Plains* avoided this 'Zero' by a hard turn to starboard and her only damage was caused by splinters.

ABOVE RIGHT: 25 October 1944: *St Lo* slows to a stop shortly after she is hit. Unable to destroy or dodge her assailant, she was doomed by the uncontrollable fires which the 'Zero's' bomb started in her hangar.

RIGHT: 1120, 25 October 1944: the explosion of torpedoes stowed in the hangar blows off the *St Lo's* stern.

small fires started by the shower of blazing gasoline from the *kamikaze*.

The fifth 'Zero' carried out a copy-book attack from astern releasing its 550lb bomb in a shallow dive before crashing into the flight deck of the *St Lo*, the only undamaged carrier in the unit. The impact of the fighter was not serious, for it slid up the deck and over the bows, but the bomb exploded in the hangar and set fire to the aircraft and the gasoline fuel system. Weapons in the hangar – depth-charges, bombs and torpedoes – 'cooked off' in the blaze and seven or eight heavy explosions set the carrier on fire throughout her length and opened her to the sea. The *St Lo* was abandoned and the remaining destroyer escorts (DEs) left the carriers to pick up survivors.

At 1110, when the burning *St Lo* was about six miles astern, a formation of enemy aircraft was sighted, having managed to approach to within five miles without ever being detected by radar. There was no time to vector fighters to intercept and the four carriers had to depend upon their own 40mm and 20mm AA guns for defense against 15 'Judies.' The majority of the dive-bombers delivered conventional attacks and made good their escapes, but at least three improvised suicide attacks. The *Kitkun Bay* was again singled out but shot down her assailant, which crashed short and sprayed her with splinters, but the *Kalinin Bay* attracted two 'Judies.' Already badly damaged, with her main steering gear

out of action and extensive flooding amidships as the result of a dozen shell hits, she was struck on the flight deck by the first aircraft. Almost simultaneously, a second 'Judy' hit the port after funnel. The latter hit caused little damage, and while the first holed the deck and started a fire, it did not penetrate to the hangar and the fire was quickly extinguished; damage to the flight deck was nevertheless severe. Ten minutes after the *Kalinin Bay* put out her fires, the *St Lo*, still blazing, capsized and sank by the stern, 30 miles east of Samar Island. Japanese gunnery and suicide aircraft had taken 1075 lives in Task Units 77.4.1 and .3 and another 1150 men were rescued from the water during the next 36 hours.

The US Navy now knew that it was facing a deliberate campaign of suicide attacks – the number of undamaged aircraft which had dived on the carriers on 25 October left no room for doubt that they might be, in more conventional terms, the last acts of doomed pilots. What was not clear was the likely scale of future operations. In the meantime, a complete news embargo was placed on the success, and even the existence of the *kamikazes*. Tactically, the short-term defensive measures could only be heightened radar and visual watchfulness and the strengthening of fighter combat air patrols to cover a wider band of heights from sea-level upward. Admiral Halsey preferred more direct offensive measures and struck at airfields where the *kamikazes* were thought to be based. Unfortunately, he had only six carriers to cover the Philippines and lack of sufficient aircraft and bad weather was to give the JNAF and JAAF opportunities to make good losses with aircraft from Formosa.

The JNAF organization on the Philippines was amended on 26 October. Vice-Admiral Fukudome assumed command of the First Air Fleet as well as his own Second, Ohnishi becoming the Chief of Staff of the 1st Combined Base Air Force. The Second Air Fleet units, which had up to now operated conventionally, were made available for *kamikaze* operations, but required some re-training, as did the replacement pilots who began to arrive for the First Air Fleet.

The original '*Shimpu* Unit' had virtually shot its bolt on 25 October, and its last mission began during the forenoon of the following day. At midday, the *kamikazes* made a coordinated attack with a dozen 'Judies' of the 761st Air Group on the escort carriers of TU.77.4.1. The dive-bombers made for the damaged *Santee*, but were beaten off by the Hellcats of the CAP. While the fighters were thus occupied, the

'Zeroes' attacked the other carriers, near-missing the *Sangamon* and *Petrof Bay* but hitting the patched-up *Suwanee*. The *kamikaze* landed square on a torpedo-bomber on the carrier's forward elevator and the fuel in both aircraft exploded, setting fire to nine other aircraft on deck; by the time that the fire was extinguished several hours later, 150 men had died and over 100 were injured. The *Suwanee* and *Santee* withdrew for repairs at the end of the day. They had both survived primarily because their damage-control teams were well-trained and dedicated, but these ships, sisters of the *Sangamon*, converted from oil tankers, were far more rugged than the purpose-built Kaiser class 'jeep carriers' which were to take the majority of hits on escort carriers.

There was a lull of four days before the JNAF suicide aircraft returned in strength. In the meantime, the light cruiser *Denver* sustained minor damage on 28 October when a JAAF fighter-bomber near-missed her in Leyte Gulf and on the next day the *Intrepid* became the first fast carrier victim of a *kamikaze* when a lone 'Zero' flew into a 20mm AA gun mounting on her deck edge – damage was slight, but 10 men were killed. This attack introduced a new *kamikaze* tactic, the 'Zero' approaching under cover of a returning strike, its radar echo indistinguishable from those of the 'friendlies.'

ABOVE: The Quad Forty, two twin 40mm Bofors guns on a single mounting, firing up to 400 2-pound shells per minute, was one of the more effective anti-suicide aircraft weapons and was widely fitted on ships down to destroyer size.

ABOVE: Noon, 26 October 1944: a fireball envelopes the forward flight deck of *Suwanee* as a 'Zero' crashes on to a parked Avenger; a second 'Zero' is passing down the carrier's starboard side, pursued by a Grumman Avenger torpedo-bomber.

The fast carriers came under attack again on 30 October. Task Group 38.4, with two large and two light carriers, was supporting the army ashore on Leyte when, during the afternoon, a raid was detected. The fighter-direction officer assumed that the enemy was attempting to approach 'under the radar' and sent the only available CAP division out at low level. Unfortunately, the six 'Zeroes' were at 18,000 feet and they were able to descend on their targets opposed only by AA gunfire. Both the *Franklin* and the light carrier *Belleau Wood* received direct hits. Both were preparing to fly off aircraft and serious fires were started, 33 aircraft being destroyed in the former and a dozen in the latter. The bomb from the *Franklin*'s *kamikaze* exploded in the carrier's hangar, causing severe damage and explosions in the ship's gasoline fuel system, but her casualties – 56 dead – were less than those of the smaller ship, which lost 92 men and had another 54 seriously injured. The two ships were too badly damaged to continue operations and the Task Group withdrew, leaving just one other fast carrier group (TG 38.2) on the line.

This withdrawal represented a major success for the *kamikazes*. The fast carrier task force off the Philippines had been reduced by fatigue and casualties to just one fast carrier and two light carriers, one of which was configured for night operations (the *Independence*). That they were there at all was due to unexpected delays in preparing an airfield ashore to permit US Army Air Force fighters and tactical bombers to take over defensive and interdiction tasks. The three carriers could make no more than a token contribution to the support of the troops and were scarcely able to defend themselves against determined air attack. A month later they, too, would be knocked off the line.

On Leyte, the US Army had secured sufficient ground for the inshore gunfire support fleet to be reduced to seven major ships and 13 destroyers. An airstrip became operational on 31 October and the USAAF flew in a wing of Lockheed P-38 Lightning fighters and a squadron of Northrop P-61 Black Widow night-fighters; neither type was particularly suitable for the task of catching highly agile suicide aircraft at low level. Despite heavy losses, Japanese aircraft, JNAF and JAAF, were present in the Philippines in greater numbers than had been available on the eve of the invasion, and the second batch of *kamikazes* had finished their tactical training. More numerous than their predecessors, they had the example of the latter's successes, exaggerated by their superiors, to spur them on.

The Japanese Navy attempted to reduce US Navy strength in Leyte Gulf by means of

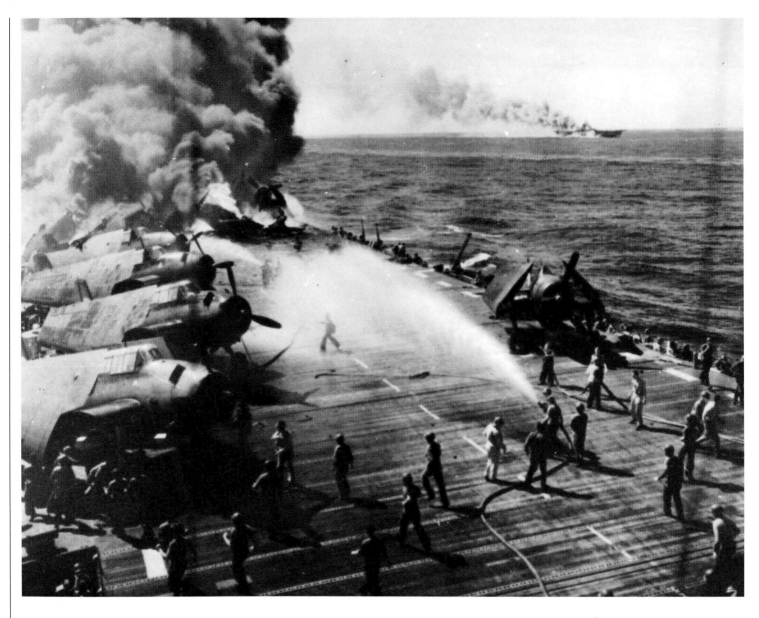

a coordinated surface and air operation, in which destroyers were sent out into the Mindanao Sea as bait to lure American ships into the narrow waters of the Surigao Straits, where they would be attacked by *kamikazes*. The US Navy knew where the destroyers were, but had insufficient ships to make the move that the Japanese wanted. As it was obvious by midday that the plan had failed, the suicide aircraft came into Leyte Gulf, where the destroyers came under attack for want of bigger targets. Half a dozen were attacked, of which three suffered near-miss damage – the *Claxton* sustained severe splinter damage, internal damage from the shock of a bomb exploding under water and 29 casualties, while the *Ammen* lost her fore funnel and part of the after funnel to a 'Zero' which missed her bridge and mast by a very narrow margin. The *Abner Read* took a direct hit, uncontrollable gasoline fires reached her after magazines, which exploded, and she capsized and sank half an hour after the attack. Forty-four men lost their lives and 53 were injured.

The JNAF husbanded its resources after this strike, waiting for more lucrative targets. The JAAF carried out destructive conventional bombing raids on the airfield within the beachhead on 2 November and the return of the Fast Carrier Task Force was urgently requested to save what appeared to be to the US Army a critical situation. Three task groups arrived on 5 November and struck at airfields and shipping in the northern Philippines for two days, claiming to have destroyed over 400 Japanese aircraft. The *kamikazes* found the task force on the afternoon of the 5th and four 'Zeroes' concentrated on the *Lexington*. Three missed or were shot down, and the fourth hit the after end of the carrier's island. The damage was superficial and did not interrupt flying, but 50 men died and 132 were hurt.

The carrier strikes had the desired effect. A week passed before the next *kamikaze* attack, which damaged two small repair ships (converted LSTs) in Leyte Gulf on 12 November, but again the Japanese air forces were given a respite to restore their

ABOVE: 30 October 1944: in their first successful attack on the fast carriers, the *kamikazes* succeed in putting *Franklin* and *Belleau Wood* out of action for weeks.

ABOVE RIGHT: 1253, 25 November 1944: a fireball of gasoline and burning debris is thrown up by the bomb carried by the first 'Zero' to hit *Intrepid*.

RIGHT: 1 November 1944: the destroyers off Leyte come under attack and a column of black smoke rises above the burning *Abner Read*; to her left, a smaller white column marks the *Anderson*.

strength, for the carriers concentrated on the shipping which was being used to supply the defenders of Leyte, via the west coast port of Ormoc. On 19 November, the carrier aircraft returned to the airfields, where over 100 aircraft were claimed as destroyed. The *kamikazes* attempted to strike back but the 11 raids, all by small numbers of aircraft, were unsuccessful – few aircraft got past the CAP and all missed the ships.

In spite of the experience of late October, the Fast Carrier Task Force was again reduced to two groups on 20 November. Again there were insufficient fighters for simultaneous offensive and defensive tasks and Admiral Halsey made the mistake of operating for several days in the same area to the east of Luzon despite the near-continuous dawn-to-dusk presence of JNAF shadowers. Task Groups 38.1 and 38.2 paid for this temerity early in the afternoon of 25 November, when two groups of *kamikazes* approached from the south. The offensive fighter sweeps had been unable to cover the airfields in southern Luzon, the reduced CAP could not destroy all the attackers and at least a dozen 'Zeroes' and 'Judies' got through to attack the ships over a period of 25 minutes. Four of the seven carriers sustained damage. The *Essex* and *Hancock*, both of TG.38.1, were able to continue operating normally, although the former lost 15 men killed.

A larger and more deadly formation fell upon TG.38.2, putting both of its day-operations carriers out of action. The *Cabot's* flight deck was holed, her catapult was damaged by a direct hit and she suffered underwater damage from a near-miss. Two direct hits on the *Intrepid* started fires which burned for over two hours and gutted her hangar. To crown TG.38.2's misfortunes, the night carrier *Independence* was damaged in a separate incident by one of her own aircraft, which crashed and caught fire on landing. With no intact carriers left, and having lost 107 men dead to enemy

action, the group withdrew. TG.38.1 remained in the Philippines area but played no further part in the Leyte campaign.

Although the JNAF's suicide aircraft had again made an important contribution by driving off the fast carriers to impotent arm's length, it did not measurably benefit the Japanese Army fighting on Leyte. Inshore, in the Gulf, the army and navy aircraft – suicide and conventional – made most of their attacks between dusk and dawn but were surprisingly unsuccessful against the stationary assault ships, damaging only two, the *Alpine* (on 17 November) and the *James O'Hara* (23rd). On the 27th, however, *kamikazes* took advantage of bad weather to attack in the late forenoon. About 25 aircraft reached the anchorage and eight scored hits or damaging near-misses on a battleship (*Colorado*), two cruisers (*St Louis* and *Montpelier*) and sinking the small sub-

BELOW: 25 November 1944: firefighters work amid the smoke and steam rising through *Intrepid*'s flight deck from her hangar fires.

RIGHT: 25 November 1944: a late-model 'Judy,' streaming gasoline vapor from a damaged wing tank, dives on the *Essex*; the pilot misjudged his dive and struck the far deck-edge, inflicting little damage before he crashed into the sea.

sufficient advantage was taken of the absence or weakness of the latter to strike at shipping in Leyte Gulf, where the attackers held all the advantages of bad weather and poor radar operating conditions (due to the proximity of land) which permitted surprise attacks. The attacks on 27 and 29 November damaged two out of the four battleships, two out of five cruisers and two out of 16 destroyers deployed in the Gulf – similar effectiveness from more frequent attacks during November would have inflicted losses which the US Navy could not easily have sustained. By the end of the month decisive success was beyond the *kamikazes'* reach; they were even more destructive in December, but the Americans' moment of greatest weakness was past.

This was not apparent to Vice-Admiral Ohnishi, who, desperate to rebuild his special attack corps, flew to Tokyo in mid-month to beg for more pilots and aircraft. Despite the obvious reluctance of Combined Fleet, he was allocated 150 aircraft – half the number requested – from training bases in Japan and Korea. Few of their pilots had more than 100 hours flying experience, but 140 aircraft managed to arrive in Taiwan toward the end of November to begin in-doctrination and training for suicide missions. This, the largest single reinforcement, began to reach the Luzon airfields at the beginning of the second week in December 1944.

BELOW: 25 November 1944: a salvage party manhandles the wreckage of a Hellcat in *Intrepid*'s gutted hangar.

marine-chaser *SC-744*. Two days later, at dusk, another raid attacked a convoy as it left the Gulf and inflicted extensive damage on the battleship *Maryland* and the destroyer *Aulick*, each of which lost 31 men killed. The destroyer *Saufley*, shock-damaged by a near-miss, suffered no major casualties.

It had taken the 1st Naval Base Air Force a month to realize that the inshore campaign was the more important, so obsessed was its staff with the American carrier fleet. In-

BY the end of November 1944, the vastly-outnumbered Japanese Army still controlled two enclaves on Leyte, one of which centered on the port of Ormoc. To overcome the dogged ground resistance in the latter area, a relatively minor amphibious operation was mounted, but this unprogrammed event obliged the US commanders (Admiral Nimitz and General MacArthur) to delay the next major operation by 10 days and the one after that (the invasion of Luzon) by 20 days. The postponement gave the Japanese air forces a respite in which they could build up their suicide and conventional strength, but it also allowed the US Navy carrier commanders a breathing space to evolve and test anti-suicide tactics.

The USAAF tactical bombers could do nothing to check the revival of Japanese air strength and they had proved unable to pre-vent the arrival of resupply convoys which enabled the Japanese to continue fighting against 6:1 odds. In early December US Marine Air Group 61 arrived on Leyte with 85 Vought F4U Corsairs which could be used as defensive fighters, for shipping strikes and close support of the army, and a dozen North American PBJ-1 Mitchell light bombers which differed from their USAAF B-25 counterparts in being armed with a 75mm gun for anti-shipping work. Accompanying MAG 61 were a dozen radar-equipped F6F-5N Hellcat night-fighters, which replaced the ineffective USAAF Black Widows.

With efficient air support, the US Army and Navy could mount an offensive seaborne hook against Ormoc and on 5 December the first landing craft convoys left Leyte. The first dawn attack on the amphibious forces was beaten off by the Marine night-fighters, but later in the forenoon an army suicide formation of eight aircraft managed to elude the USAAF Lightning CAP and struck at a group of Landing Ships (Medium) as they left Surigao Straits. *LSM.20* took a direct hit and sank in flames and *LSM.23* was hit by a fighter which bounced off the water and into her side, causing only superficial damage. Six hours later, JNAF *kamikazes* from Cebu attacked another convoy as it entered the straits and hit two destroyers, the *Mugford* and *Drayton*. A 'Zero' caused a serious fire forward of the latter's bridge but, like the Aichi 'Val' which hit at the base of the *Mugford*'s funnel, it failed to penetrate the upper deck and damage was slight. Casualties were light, for only 22 men were killed and 30 injured in the four vessels hit on this day.

The US Army landed in Ormoc Bay on 7 December and the suicide units reacted in force, beginning with a double success. At

CHAPTER 3

ORMOC AND MINDORO

0945, eight *kamikazes*, escorted by six fighters, brushed aside the outnumbered Lightning CAP and concentrated on the destroyer *Mahan* and the 'fast transport' (APD) *Ward*. The latter, a small, old destroyer rebuilt to carry and land a company of troops, was hit in the forward boiler room and sank quickly after an internal explosion, though with no loss of life. The *Mahan* claimed that nine *kamikazes* had attacked her. Three of these hit her, one at the rear of the bridge and one above the waterline on each side of the ship, just forward of the bridge, starting uncontrollable fires. Abandoned 40 minutes after the attack, the *Mahan* was scuttled by USS *Walke*.

Another raid, shortly before midday, saw four 'Zeroes' break through to attack the fast transport *Liddle* (a destroyer escort conversion). Three of these missed, one sufficiently near to cause underwater splinter damage, but the last hit her bridge, destroying the crowded Combat Information Center, where most of the 58 casualties (36 fatal) occurred. The *Liddle* was in no danger of sinking, but a surprise attack by a single aircraft in mid-afternoon reduced the destroyer *Lamson* to a derelict, killing 21 of her crew and injuring 50 others. Hit on the rear of the bridge and set on fire by the aircraft and its load of small bombs, she came to a standstill with a flooded boiler room and was abandoned. Orders were given to scuttle her but these were canceled and she was towed back to Leyte. In the Surigao Straits, *LST.737* shrugged off a *kamikaze* hit to continue her return, empty, to Leyte. The Japanese suffered even more severely at sea, as the Marine Corsairs sank all five ships of an Ormoc-bound convoy.

The Army Air Force fighters had been handicapped throughout the day. The patrols were not strong enough to deal with large raids, let alone to get rid of the shadowers and investigate the decoys which the Japanese used to divert the attention of the defenses. The landlocked bay interfered with radar, so that detection was frequently too late for an interception, but equally unfortunate was the USAAF's pilots' lack of experience of the naval methods of close control of fighter patrols. To be fair to the Lightning pilots, the naval fighter controllers were themselves only just beginning to get to grips with the problems which *kamikaze* tactics had created.

After the repeated attacks on 5 and 7 December there was a brief lull as the *kamikaze* units equipped with fighter and dive-bomber types were brought to their maximum strength to prepare for the defense of Luzon, which Imperial Headquarters and Combined Fleet believed to be the next major target. In the meantime, torpedo-bomber units were sent into the Ormoc battle.

The twin-engined Mitsubishi 'Betties' made a dramatic debut on the evening of 11 December, when they attacked a convoy to the east of the Surigao Straits. Eight aircraft attacked and five scored direct hits, sinking the merchant Liberty ship *William S Ladd* and the Landing Craft (Tank) *LCT.1075* outright. The motor torpedo boat *PT.323* was apparently mistaken for bigger prey, for two of the 15-ton aircraft hit her. Miraculously, she survived long enough to beach herself on a nearby island, where she was abandoned. The destroyer *Hughes* also survived the impact of one of these big aircraft and the explosion of its bombs, to be towed back to Leyte with severe damage and flooded machinery spaces.

Twenty-four hours later, 10 Nakajima 'Jill' carrier torpedo-bombers, operating from

shore bases, hit an Ormoc convoy off the west end of the straits. Half a dozen attacked with torpedoes, all of which missed, and the damage was done by the bomb-armed *kamikazes*. The destroyer *Caldwell* suffered minor damage from a near miss and continued with the convoy, but two 'Jills' flew into the *Reid* in quick succession, hitting her under the bridge and right aft. The bomb from the second aircraft carried forward and exploded over the five-inch magazine, which in turn detonated, opening the ship to the sea. The *Reid*, already heeling to starboard as she turned hard to port, never came back to the upright, but continued to roll to starboard until she reached her beam ends and sank, two minutes after the explosions. One hundred and fifty men were lost, the heaviest toll since the loss of the *St Lo*, but some of these were accounted for by the surviving 'Jills,' which strafed the survivors in the water.

TOP: Mitsubishi 'Betty' torpedo-bombers in their element at very low level, seen here attacking invasion shipping off Guadalcanal in August 1942.

ABOVE: 10 December 1944: the motor torpedo-boat *PT.323*, cut in half by one of the 'Betties' which hit her, lies beached off an island at the eastern entrance to the Surigao Strait.

The arrival of a division of Corsairs put an end to this activity – three Japanese aircraft were shot down and the others driven off.

The final *kamikaze* attack of the Ormoc campaign was another mixed raid, delivered early on 12 December, against the same convoy that had been attacked at dusk the previous evening and was now returning to Leyte. The *Caldwell*, which had then escaped serious damage, now sustained a direct hit which wrecked the bridge, killing 33 men and starting fires. The 'Zero's' bomb exploded near the forward (No 1) five-inch gun and a few minutes later another bomb, dropped by a conventional attacker, exploded in the superstructure under No 2 gun. Severely damaged, the *Caldwell* was able to make her own way back to Leyte.

The week-long Ormoc *kamikaze* campaign cost the JNAF at least 50 suicide aircraft. They had sunk six ships (and wrecked an MTB) and damaged seven others more or less severely and had thus achieved a respectable rate of striking. But however satisfying the statistics may have appeared (and the Japanese commanders believed them to be even more favorable), they represented no major achievement. The absence of the fast carriers had allowed the suicide units to operate unhindered from bases close to their targets and the shipping had not been well protected against air attack. Strategically, Leyte was already doomed and it was not the Ormoc losses which delayed the capture of the port (which fell on Christmas Day) but the endurance of the Japanese Army, which alone had forced a postponement of the American timetable.

The strategic program had resumed a momentum which could not be checked by even the accumulation of minor attrition which was all that the Ormoc suicide attacks could hope to achieve. Even as the US Ormoc convoys were taking their final hits, ships bound for the next major operation were underway – the 1st Base Air Force would have been better advised to conserve its aircraft and dedicated young men for a more important campaign.

The next American objective was the island of Mindoro, which was required for its airfield sites from which land-based tactical bombers could reach the Manila area and fighters could protect shipping bound for the west coast of Luzon, the main objective in the overall Philippines campaign. The advance was the shortest since the Central Pacific campaign had begun a year previously, for the intended beachhead, in the vicinity of San Jose, was only 260 miles from the nearest of the Leyte airfields, but the distance was still too great for Leyte-based aircraft to provide continuous dawn-to-dusk defensive patrols, and carrier fighters would be needed to cover the passage of the assault convoys and during the initial stages of the landings.

The close covering force for the Mindoro operation included six escort carriers, each with 24 Grumman FM-2 Wildcat fighters embarked instead of the hitherto standard complement of 16 fighters, an increase made possible by a reduction in the number of Grumman TBM-1 Avenger torpedo-bombers. The carriers would be capable of maintaining 12 fighters on patrol at all times, with a minimum of 12 more at immediate

BELOW: The Nakajima 'Jill' was originally introduced as a torpedo-bomber but, equipped with radar (as in this picture), was more widely used as a scout and shadower for suicide raids than as a *kamikaze* aircraft.

readiness on deck, awaiting the order to 'scramble' on detection of a raid. Also in the covering force were three old battleships, three light cruisers and no fewer than 18 destroyers. There would be no repetition of the Samar surface battle between capital ships and ill-protected escort carriers.

Distant cover, as before, was the task of Halsey's Third Fleet, and particularly the Fast Carrier Task Force commanded by Vice-Admiral J S McCain. Two large carriers and one light carrier were repairing *kamikaze* damage, another large carrier was being converted for night operations and, with the loss of the *Princeton*, only seven large and five light carriers, plus the night-flying *Independence*, were available. These were formed into three task groups, instead of the usual four, to increase the defensive power of each group. The strength varied, but the 'weakest,' TG.38.1, comprised four carriers, with 156 Hellcat fighters and 144 attack aircraft embarked, two modern battleships, four cruisers and 18 destroyers.

The 10-day 'rest' caused by the delays on Leyte was the longest enjoyed by the fast carriers for five months. It was put to good use by McCain and his staff, in particular the veteran fighter tactician Commander Jimmy Thach who studied Japanese methods so far employed and devised and tested measures to counter suicide attacks. These took account of the known weaknesses in the US Navy's system and equipment – weaknesses which were by now known to the Japanese as well – and resulted in a revised defensive organization intended to destroy as many attackers as possible.

To extend the radar horizon against *kamikazes* approaching at low level, each task group disposed up to six of its destroyers between some 30 and 60 miles up-threat, that is, in the direction from which attacks were expected, of the carriers. These 'Tomcat' pickets were allocated their own fighter CAP, which had the dual task of interception under the direction of fighter controllers in the destroyers and of 'delousing' returning friendly strikes, to sort out *kamikazes* attempting to appear as additional radar echoes in a stream of contacts. To ease the fighters' job, certain destroyers were nominated as 'gates,' through which all returning strike formations should pass for visual identification.

For close-range air defense of the task groups, the standing fighter patrols were increased in strength and, instead of holding at an altitude of about 20,000 feet over the force, were split between a 'HiCAP' above 25,000 feet 40 miles up-threat and a 'Med-CAP' above 10,000 feet 20 miles up-threat. With adequate radar warning, they would be able to make the initial interceptions well away from the task group and the MedCAPs could be replaced by fighters scrambled from immediate readiness on deck.

A completely new patrol – the 'Jack CAP' – was formed for last-ditch defense against the low-level surprise *kamikazes* which had managed to sneak undetected past the pickets or had dived to evade the high-level CAPs. Four fighters orbited at low level (below 3000 feet) on each of four stations (north, east, south and west) 5000 yards beyond each task group's destroyer screen. These fighters were not controlled by the radar fighter direction organization but by visual controllers in the destroyers and they were not intended to pursue *kamikazes* within AA range of the ships. Gunfire was more effective as the result of the provision of a higher proportion of radar-proximity fuzes for five-inch shells. Triggered by the target, these fuzes enabled the big AA guns to be used for accurate, deliberately aimed fire, rather than predicted barrage fire, converting many near misses into 'kills.'

The task groups were to operate within supporting range of one another. Not only did this mean that an endangered group could call upon fighters from an unthreatened neighbor, but the disposition also reduced two of the biggest shortcomings of their relatively low-frequency long-range warning radar. Beside the well-known gap at low level, there were others at medium heights due to transmission characteristics which produced a series of vertical 'lobes.' While maximum detection

BELOW: December 1944: Task Group 58.2, with the light carrier *Independence* leading the *Lexington* and the battleships *New Jersey*, *Iowa* and *Wisconsin*, leaves Ulithi to support the Mindoro landings.

range could even be as great as 200 miles against a formation of aircraft at certain heights, in the gaps between the lobes this range would be more than halved and if aircraft managed to stay in the gap by descending toward the transmitter they might not be detected at all, for the minimum range of the radar could be as little as 20 miles in rough seas. The other short-range deficiency of the warning radar was its lack of overhead coverage – once through the lobes, aircraft were virtually undetectable in a 'cone of silence.' By overlapping the radars of adjacent task groups, the gaps caused by the lobes were virtually eliminated (for they were a function of range) and the blank arc in a task group's overhead was covered by its neighbor's radar. One ship, the new *Ticonderoga* in TG 38.3, took a more positive approach and fitted an APS-4 radar, taken from an Avenger torpedo-bomber, on the island, mounted vertically to search the zenith for the diving *kamikazes*.

McCain's staff also introduced Exercise Moosetrap, a *kamikaze* simulation by one task group to test the others' air defenses, probing for weaknesses in the new tactics and their execution. Moosetrap showed up the need for greater flexibility on the part of fighter controllers, particularly in handing over 'their' CAPs to other controllers who were better placed to make effective use of the fighters. It also demonstrated the need for very tight radio discipline for, with few frequencies available, and large numbers of fighters on the primary defense channel, 'cutting-in' on essential warnings and orders was a constant source of danger and total congestion a very real possibility.

Having improved the defensive arrangements, the staff concentrated on the main method of defeating the Japanese air forces – offensive strikes and sweeps to catch them on the ground or in the air near their bases. Thach planned a system of continuous daylight patrols over the Luzon airfields which became known as 'The Big Blue Blanket'; by night, the *Independence*'s aircraft would interdict the same airfields to dissuade the JNAF from attempting night attacks on any shipping. Thus prepared, the Fast Carrier Task Force sailed from Ulithi on 11 December and headed for an operating position off the east of Luzon, where it would begin operations on 14 December, the day before the Mindoro assault.

The Mindoro invasion fleet was meanwhile already at sea, the close cover having sailed from the Palaus as early as 5 December. Japanese reconnaissance aircraft sighted the amphibious attack ships on the 13th as they passed to the south of the Visayan group of islands and into the Sulu Sea. There were by now few *kamikaze* aircraft left on the airfields in the Visayas and it was not until mid-afternoon that the first raid took off.

The *kamikazes* found the amphibious group south of Negros Island at 1500. The Wildcats from the escort carriers and a Corsair CAP from Leyte intercepted but were not able to stop one 'Val' from diving on and hitting the flagship, the light cruiser *Nashville*, amidships. The impact caused little structural damage but the inevitable fire caused heavy loss of life among the exposed AA guns' crews and two 145-pound bombs bounced off the deck and exploded in mid-air, inflicting further personnel casualties. One hundred and thirty officers and men died and 190 were injured, the casualties including senior officers of the naval and military HQ staffs. As the cruiser's operations room and communications had been badly damaged by bomb fragments, the surviving staff officers transferred to another ship and the group sailed on.

Two hours later, a raid from Cebu, made up of three *kamikazes* escorted by seven fighters, found and attacked the covering group to the southwest of Negros. Only one aircraft got past the CAP and the pilot settled for an attack on the screen, hitting the *Haraden* on the forward funnel. The destroyer came to a stop, her forward boiler room severely damaged and with aviation fuel blazing on her upper deck, but she was soon under way once more, heading for Leyte with 14 men dead and 24 injured.

Over 60 JNAF and JAAF suicide aircraft

BELOW: Aichi 'Val' dive-bombers, obsolete by 1944, were still available in large numbers for *kamikaze* attacks and were thus employed in all the campaigns from Leyte to Okinawa.

took off on at least three separate missions against the Mindoro expedition on 14 December. Not one Japanese attack aircraft was seen by any of the ships at sea. The biggest single mission, a composite raid by 29 JAAF and 40 JNAF aircraft (nearly 50 of them intending suicide), was caught while forming up over Clark Field, near Manila, by the first 'Big Blue Blanket' sweep of the day. The Hellcats shot down over 40 aircraft in this battle and the few suiciders which got away and persisted with their task were caught and destroyed by the escort carriers' Wildcats. The latter had a field day, for they were equally successful against the later small-scale *kamikaze* attacks and a number of reconnaissance aircraft and shadowers which appeared around the amphibious group. The Marine Corsairs from Leyte extended the blanket over Masbate, Cebu and Bohol, allowing the Wildcats time for an offensive sweep of their own against *kamikaze* bases on Panay and Negros Islands.

The fast carriers flew over 1600 sorties on 14 December. Beside the scrap over Clark Field, there was only one other major battle over Luzon, when eight Hellcats from the *Ticonderoga*, patrolling over Vigan, northeast Luzon, sighted and intercepted a gaggle of 27 'Zeroes' and army Nakajima 'Oscars.' Only seven of the Japanese aircraft, which were apparently reinforcements flying in from Formosa, escaped and not one of the Hellcats was lost.

The US Army landings on Mindoro were unopposed. At 0800 on 15 December, half an hour after 'H-Hour,' USAAF Lightnings took responsibility for beachhead CAP and the escort carriers began their scheduled withdrawal. Ten minutes later, the first *kamikaze* raid appeared, directed at the covering group. Three aircraft got past the Wildcats: a Nakajima 'Kate' torpedo-bomber which broke up under automatic AA fire but parts of whose wreckage fell aboard the destroyer *Ralph Talbot*, and two 'Zeroes' which nearmissed the carrier *Marcus Island*, clipping the edge of the flight deck. These were the first of a score of aircraft which attacked over a 45-minute period, dividing their attention between the covering and amphibious groups.

Direct hits were scored on two tank landing ships which were standing off, awaiting their turn to unload. *LST.472* and *LST.738* were hit and abandoned after fires had started a chain of explosions among the cargo of both vessels. Loss of life was light (only nine men) but the LSTs had to be scuttled by destroyer gunfire and the loss of their vehicles was serious. The destroyer *Howorth* also lost nine men when a 'Zero'

crashed through her gun director tower on top of the bridge but inflicted no other serious damage. The MTB *PT.223* was slightly damaged by a near miss. The final small raid, at 0900, was driven off by the *Savo Island*'s Wildcats. Thereafter, the amphibious group proceeded to unload without hindrance and made such good progress that the surviving LSTs were able to withdraw at dusk on the 15th. The escort carriers' withdrawal was postponed and they remained to provide the dawn patrol on the 16th.

The fast carriers' 'Big Blue Blanket' over Luzon had prevented all but the first strike on the 15th and it was spread again on the next day. On their way inbound for the first sweep the fighters from the *Lexington* and *Hancock* met a raid outbound for the car-

LEFT: Repair work begins at Puget Sound Navy Yard on the destroyer *Haraden*, damaged by a *kamikaze* on 13 December 1944.

BELOW: 5 December 1944: the landing ship *LSM.20* sinks following a suicide attack.

riers and destroyed all 11 *kamikazes* – no further attempts were made to attack the fleet. At the end of the day, the fast carriers and their screens withdrew to refuel as scheduled. Off Mindoro, the escort carriers had to be retained for a further day as bad weather over Leyte on 16 December prevented land-based fighters from operating. A number of small suicide raids occurred, but most were broken up and driven off by the Wildcats and the few aircraft which persisted scored no hits on the shipping.

The *kamikaze* corps was named after 'the divine wind' – the typhoon which in 1281 had saved Japan by destroying the fleet supporting Kublai Khan's Mongol army, thus cutting off the invaders' supplies. The modern-day technical *kamikazes* had come nowhere near such an achievement, but nature, aided by Admiral Halsey's poor judgment, did its best to repeat history. The rain and low cloud which had 'weathered-out' Leyte on 16 December were the distant effects of a typhoon which hit Task Force 38 and its replenishment groups on 17 December and reached its peak on the next day. Three destroyers foundered, with the loss of

over 800 men, and among the many ships damaged were four of the six light carriers – among the 143 aircraft lost were all of the *Monterey*'s, blown overboard or written off in a serious hangar fire. The postponed replenishment took place on 19 and 20 December and the operation as a whole was abandoned on the 21st, when the Fast Carrier Task Force set course for Ulithi.

The 'divine wind' might have driven the main striking force back to base, but the US Army could still rely upon the navy to do its best to resupply Mindoro and the distant effects of the storm prevented *kamikaze* operations from the main Luzon bases. Few attacks were attempted up to 21 December. On the 17th three suicide aircraft ganged up on *PT.84* but could only damage her by their near misses, while a fourth just missed the beached *LST.605* and plowed into the sand. The PT boats came under attack again on the 18th, and this time all but one of the crew of *PT.300* were either killed or wounded by a direct hit which sank the boat.

Japanese Army aircraft found a resupply convoy about 55 miles south of Mindoro in

the late afternoon of 21 December and a strong mixed raid of conventional bombers and suicide fighter-bombers was sent out. The land-based CAP destroyed five of the latter but of eight which got through a Nakajima 'Tojo' near-missed the destroyer *Foote*, causing underwater damage, and three 'Oscars' hit LSTs *.460* and *.749* and the merchant ship *Juan de Fuca*, setting fire to all three ships. The gasoline and ammunition aboard *LST.460* exploded and she sank rapidly; *LST.749*'s crew had her fires almost under control but the distraction of an attack by conventional bombers (which missed) led to the flames gaining a fresh hold and she was abandoned. Total casualties aboard the LSTs included 107 men killed. The SS *Juan de Fuca* extinguished her fires and, although she straggled from the convoy, she managed to reach Mindoro. The ships were again attacked by JAAF suicide aircraft on 22 December, after arrival at Mindoro, but they came close only to two destroyers, the *Bryant* and *Newcomb*, which received superficial damage from splinters.

Thereafter, the Mindoro anchorage was left alone by suicide aircraft for over a week, the Japanese in the Visayas having at last learned to bide their time until a worthwhile target appeared. Those on Luzon had other problems, for on 22 December USAAF four-engined bombers began a series of heavy and destructive raids on the airfields in the Manila and Clark Field area. These proved to be the final straw as far as Imperial Headquarters was concerned and, effectively, marked the end of the reinforcement of the JNAF and JAAF in the Philippines.

The suitable target for the waiting suicide aircraft appeared on 28 December, having sailed on the previous day from Leyte Gulf. The resupply convoy consisted of over 90 landing craft, tenders and PT boats but only nine large cargo vessels, screened by a dozen destroyers and covered by CAPs from Leyte. During the forenoon of the 28th, when the convoy was to the south of Negros, three *kamikazes* from Cebu attacked without warning, singling out the most lucrative targets to score hits on two of the three merchant Liberty ships. The *John Burke*, loaded with ammunition, blew up immediately, with the loss of all 68 men on board, but the *William Sharon* was more fortunate, for the 'Zero' failed to penetrate to the holds and the intense fire on her upper deck was extinguished before it could reach her cargo of TNT and ammunition. She was towed back to Leyte.

The convoy lost an LST to a dusk torpedo attack on the 28th but saw no action on the 29th, due mainly to the efficiency of the Mindoro-based CAP, which destroyed several formations well clear of the ships, and arrived off Mindoro on 30 December. That afternoon, five aircraft, identified as 'Vals' but probably JAAF Mitsubishi 'Sonias,' made a surprise attack on the shipping and scored four hits. The destroyer *Pringle* was hit on her after superstructure but managed to put out her fires and remain in action – her next encounter with *kamikazes* would be her last. The *Gansevoort* was hit just above the waterline and a bomb exploded in the after boiler room, flooding the space and depriving the destroyer of all power, so that her crew took an hour to extinguish the fires. A third suicider was hit by AA fire during its attack on the PT-tender *Orestes* but it ricocheted off the sea and into her side, a 550lb bomb continuing through to explode inboard; 59 men were killed by the blast and the subsequent fires, but the converted LST remained afloat.

The fourth victim was the USS *Porcupine*, a Liberty ship converted for use as a base tanker in forward areas. She was hit aft and her cargo of gasoline, intended for the PT boats and the USAAF garrison, was set on fire by the crash and the bomb explosion, but it did not itself explode, nor did it spread far forward. After the tanker had been burning for over an hour, a dubious order was given to the immobilized *Gansevoort* to attempt to blow off the damaged stern with a torpedo. The destroyer scored a hit, but it did not have the desired effect, for it spilled burning gasoline over the sea, threatening

BELOW: *Kamikaze* crews leave for their aircraft dispersal areas.

to engulf the *Gansevoort*, whose crew was ordered to abandon ship. Another vessel pulled the destroyer clear. With the *Orestes*, she was later towed to Leyte, but the *Porcupine* and her load of fuel were a total loss.

An hour after this unnecessary drama, a conventional bombing attack sank the sole surviving merchant ship of the convoy. The military situation on Mindoro was fully under control, but the supply position was suddenly becoming critical, thanks to the *kamikazes'* and bombers' success against this convoy. Another was prepared, but before it could leave Leyte the bombers hit two more Liberty ships off Mindoro and set the beached *Juan de Fuca* (*kamikazed* on 21 December) on fire.

The relief convoy left Leyte on New Year's Day 1945 and was not attacked on passage, there being bigger game afoot for the suicide aircraft, but on arrival off Mindoro on 4 January the ships were greeted by the last suicide attack of this campaign. Only one suicide aircraft got through, but it hit the merchant ship *Lewis L Dyche* and its bomb went off among the cargo of ammunition. The resulting blast killed all 71 men of her crew and seriously damaged two PT boats and *LCI.621*, which lost another three men between them.

The Mindoro anti-shipping campaign cost the Japanese approximately 200 aircraft, beside about the same number destroyed by the fast carriers. Of those lost in attacks against the invasion force and resupply convoys, 100 were expended in suicide attacks which hit, or damaged by near misses, 25 ships and craft. The JAAF suicide attackers had proved to be at least the equal of the naval *kamikazes*, the more experienced army pilots having learned rapidly from their comrades' early examples. Target selection was better than off Leyte, for of the 13 vessels sunk or very severely damaged, nine were LSTs and Liberty ships engaged in resupply, but there were still examples of mindless waste, such as the three separate attacks on PT boats. Properly directed, against suitable targets, they could have rendered the US Army's position on Mindoro sufficiently precarious to force a delay in the execution of the next American operation, the invasion of Luzon.

The US plan for the invasion of Luzon by-passed Manila and its powerfully-fortified bay. Lingayen Gulf, about 100 miles to the north of the city, was chosen because its excellent beaches gave good access to the central plain, where the best of the US-built airfields were located, and the seizure of Lingayen town would cut the main north-south road and rail communications in western Luzon. The ships and beachhead would be squeezed between counter-attacks from all the airfields in Luzon and in addition from Formosa, only 345 miles to the north and thus within easy *kamikaze* range. With the Mindoro airfields also 300 miles distant, and only the escort carriers available to provide daylight CAP until Lingayen airfield could be secured and stocked for USAAF fighters, the fast carriers, in their continuous air suppression role, would again be essential.

The first job for the fast carriers was to ensure that no reinforcements could reach Luzon from Formosa. The 11 day and two night carriers got within 140 miles (224km) of the latter undetected and on 3 and 4 January their aircraft attempted to penetrate bad weather to attack the airfields. Although they were only partly successful, over 100 Japanese aircraft were destroyed during the two days – however disappointing these results may have been, they were enough to ensure that no Formosa-based aircraft were sent south, either to reinforce the Philippine units or to deliver attacks directly. Task Force 38 then withdrew for two days to refuel, prior to spreading the 'Big Blue Blanket' over Luzon again.

The first attack on the invasion force (Task Force 77) occurred early on 3 January, as it was passing south of Negros. Three JAAF medium bombers made an unsuccessful conventional attack on the mine-sweeping group and were followed very quickly by a 'Val,' or (again, more probably), a 'Sonia,' which flew into the oiler *Cowanesque*, inflicting only very superficial damage.

Thirty-six hours elapsed before the next successful attack, thanks to the very efficient air defenses of Task Force 77. A dozen escort carriers, with 200 Wildcats between them, maintained a daylight CAP of 40 aircraft, augmented by 20 fighters from Leyte, over the armada of 157 vessels sailing in several groups spread over many miles of sea. Controlled by fighter directors in the *Natoma Bay* and *Makin Island*, the CAPs splashed a score of Japanese aircraft on the 3rd and of the few which got through, the nearest approach to a ship was by a JAAF suicide aircraft which missed the *Makin Island* by 500 yards.

There was a lull in Japanese air activity on 4 January, as Task Force 77 steamed north through the Sulu Sea toward Mindoro. At 1712, without warning, a twin-engined JAAF Kawasaki 'Nick' fighter dived on the carrier *Ommaney Bay* – only the battleship *New Mexico* had time to open fire before it crashed through the after end of the island

and into the flight deck. One of the two bombs which the 'Nick' carried exploded in the hangar but the other penetrated as far as the forward engine room, where it started an oil fire whose thick smoke quickly permeated the ship, interfering with the hangar firefighting. More serious, however, was the total loss of fire-main pressure. Despite the efforts of destroyer escorts alongside, the fires became uncontrollable and the order to abandon carrier was passed at 1750. Half an hour later, a torpedo in the hangar stowage 'cooked off' in the intense heat, killing two men in one of the DEs alongside and bringing the toll to 95 fatal casualties. Just a few minutes earlier, another suicide aircraft had missed the carrier *Lunga Point* by barely 50 yards and it was decided to abandon all attempts to save the *Ommaney Bay*, which was scuttled by the destroyer *Burns*. Fifty miles to the north, the *Lewis L Dyche* had been hit and blown up at about the time that the *Ommaney Bay* was abandoned.

By dawn on 5 January, the invasion force was within 150 miles of the airfields in the Manila area, which had yet to be attacked by the fast carriers. To make matters worse for the naval defenses, the Mindoro airfields were weathered-in and no land-based CAP would be available. Good radar warning and direction enabled the Wildcats to break up the first two raids at over 35 miles out from the force, but a third, much more determined raid of 16 *kamikazes*, escorted by four 'Zeroes,' broke through the CAP from about 1650 and damaged 10 ships in the space of 20 minutes.

Two 'Zeroes' carried out a low-level pull-up and dive attack on the carrier *Manila Bay*. One very narrowly missed but the other hit at the base of the island. The bomb exploded high in the hangar, setting fire to two aircraft, but the fire was rapidly extinguished and the carrier continued – she was capable of limited flying operations within 24 hours and by 9 January was very nearly fully efficient, although she had lost 22 men killed and 56 injured. Her sister-ship *Savo Island* avoided another *kamikaze* by skillful maneuvering and distracting the pilot by shining her searchlight full in his eyes – his wing tip still clipped the carrier's radar antenna before he crashed alongside.

Two cruisers were hit – the USS *Louisville* on the face of 'B' turret, which was severely damaged, and HMAS *Australia* right aft, where slight damage was sustained but 25 men were killed. Both remained with the force. Another Australian ship, the destroyer *Arunta*, was so narrowly missed that her steam safety valves were opened by the shock and she came to a stop, with two men dead, until steam could be restored to her turbines. The US destroyer *Helm* had her main mast and radio antenna carried away by a *kamikaze* that crashed some distance away, but the destroyer escort *Stafford* was less fortunate. Having shot down one suicide aircraft, the *Stafford* was hit amidships by the next to attack and her starboard machinery spaces were flooded. The DE was unable to keep up with the force and a tug was detached to support her, with a destroyer to guard them both until they could join a southbound convoy five days later.

The fleet tug *Apache* and the small seaplane tender *Orca* sustained minor damage

ABOVE: 1743, 6 January 1945: a *kamikaze* heads for the cruiser *Louisville*, to impact on her bridge, where Rear Admiral T E Chandler and 31 men of the ship's company died.

from glancing hits, but the support landing craft *LCI(G).70* was severely damaged and lost 10 men killed by a direct hit. Two of the escorting fighters escaped, having witnessed one of the most successful – in terms of the proportion of hits – missions of the entire suicide campaign. But however determined and accurate these Mabalacat naval pilots might have been, their sacrifice did not appreciably reduce the power or effectiveness of the invasion covering force.

The covering force divided into separate task groups during the night of 5/6 January and the fighter cover was stretched. Not only did the physical separation of the task groups make it difficult to meet any raid, but there was once again the problem of proximity to land and its effect on radar warning. Much reliance was placed upon the fast carriers for interdiction of the *kamikazes'* bases, to prevent them taking off or destroy them in the air before they came near the

gulf. Task Force 38 resumed air operations on 6 January after replenishing, turning to Luzon for the first time, and somewhat belatedly. Bad weather rendered the blanket threadbare and only 32 Japanese aircraft were destroyed. The rain and low cloud did not prevent the suicide aircraft from taking off (they were not expecting to have to land back at base) and 14 of their losses were in air combat. Many more were airborne, though, and at least 28 *kamikazes* and 15 escort fighters attacked TF 77, inflicting greater or lesser damage on 14 ships.

The escort carriers' fighters intercepted the first raid on the 6th, destroying five of the 10 aircraft involved. The surviving *kamikazes* all missed. The main suicide effort began just before midday and, by dividing their effort between the bombardment groups and the minesweeping activities 20 miles to the southward, the *kamikazes* managed to split the CAP's attention. The first to be hit was the battleship *New Mexico*, the flagship of the covering force, high on the bridge. Local blast and fire damage was severe – Vice-Admiral Oldendorf was unharmed, as was the designated commander of the British Pacific Fleet, Admiral Sir Bruce Fraser, who was along for experience of US Navy operations, but the ship's captain and Lieutenant General Sir Herbert Lumsden, Churchill's personal aide to General Mac-Arthur, were among the 30 men killed. The destroyer *Walke* shot down two *kamikazes* before she too lost her captain when struck on the bridge and the *Allen M Sumner* was hit on the after torpedo-tube mounting; unusually, there was no fire but splinters from the bomb caused her after five-inch magazine to flood. The destroyers lost 27 men killed and 59 injured between them but, like the battleship, they remained in action.

Fifteen minutes later, the minesweeping units came under attack but the only hit was on the DMS *Long*, which was hit on the side of the hull amidships by a 'Zero.' The crew, unable to control the flames, left the ship abandoned at anchor, where a fleet tug subsequently put out the fires. Only one man was lost and the remainder were picked up by the *Hovey*, a sister-ship. Another of the converted old destroyers, the APD *Brooks*, was hit and set on fire at 1252; she was abandoned but her firefighting parties, with the aid of the Australian destroyer *Warramunga*, put out all fires within 30 minutes. Loss of life was small and the survivors were transferred to the *Hovey*, while the *Warramunga* towed the *Brooks* out of the gulf. The APD was subsequently towed all the way back to Leyte, where it was decided that

BELOW: Vice Admiral Jesse B Oldendorf, commanding the Lingayen covering force, was fortunate to escape uninjured when a 'Zero' crashed into the *New Mexico*'s bridge on 6 January 1945.

LEFT: Late-model 'Zero' fighters (code-named 'Zeke 52' by the Allies) prepare for a *kamikaze* escort mission; usually out-classed by the American carrier fighters, they served more as a distraction than as protection for the suicide aircraft.

she was beyond economical repair.

Small-scale raids occurred during the afternoon, but only one of these, on the bombardment force, inflicted any damage. One *kamikaze*, streaming gasoline from damaged tanks, narrowly missed the cruiser *Columbia*, passing between her masts, but another hit the destroyer *O'Brien* on the waterline right aft. No casualties were suffered, but damage to the hull caused flooding which spread to the magazines as the ship maneuvered at high speed to avoid later attacks.

The heaviest suicide attacks came from 1720 and were directed at both areas within the gulf. The bombardment group took the first blows, five 'Zeroes' scoring a direct hit (on the battleship *California*) and two near misses (on the destroyers *Newcomb* and *Richard P Leary*). The two 'Zeroes' which failed to hit were shot down by AA fire, which also inflicted casualties and some damage on the *California*, the *Newcomb* and another destroyer, the *Lowry*.

The *California* shrugged off her direct hit, although she had lost 45 dead and 151 injured to the *kamikaze* and shell hits, but four minutes later the light cruiser *Columbia* was severely damaged when a 'Zero' crashed into her quarterdeck abreast the after six-inch turret. The aircraft's engine went through two decks and the bomb exploded deep in the ship, causing severe fires and extensive flooding. The fires were extinguished within half an hour and the cruiser, down by the stern and with her after magazines flooded, continued the bombardment with her forward guns.

Down the gulf, the damaged and abandoned *Long* was hit again and her back broke. Another converted old destroyer, the DMS *Southard*, was hit on the waterline amidships at 1732 and set on fire. Her crew, who had suffered no fatal casualties, put out the fire but she had to be towed out of the gulf. Repaired overnight, she was ready to resume sweeping on the next day.

The final raid was again on the cruisers. The *Australia* and the *Louisville* were each hit for the second time, the former on her side, amidships, and the latter on the bridge, where the explosion of the *kamikaze*'s bomb and gasoline fires killed 32 men, including the rear admiral commanding the cruiser group, and injured 56 others. The *Louisville* was unable to continue in action, but the *Australia*, with 14 more of her company dead and her speed reduced temporarily to 22 knots, remained on the line. The last ship to suffer damage on this hectic day was the heavy cruiser USS *Minneapolis*, which sustained minor damage when a

LEFT: 1724, 6 January 1945: the light cruiser *Columbia* is hit abreast her after 6-inch turrets and severely damaged by an obsolete JAAF fighter, a fixed-undercarriage Nakajima 'Nate'.

kamikaze plowed through a radar antenna on its way to crash alongside, where it scattered splinters.

Suicide aircraft, mostly naval, had hit or near-missed 21 ships on 5 and 6 January, killing 227 and injuring 633 American, British and Australian personnel. Despite the extremely high striking rate, which was the best ever achieved by suicide forces, only four ships were put out of action or forced to withdraw. No ship had been lost outright and although the *Long* foundered after daybreak on the 7th it had taken two direct hits to sink this 25-year-old 1100-ton destroyer-minesweeper.

The basic cause of the failure to inflict more serious damage lay in the nature of the aircraft employed. The Mitsubishi 'Zero' was a lightweight aircraft, with a low mass relative to its size – fully loaded, carrying a 550lb bomb, it weighed less than three tons. Seldom hitting at velocities as high as 500 feet per second (155 m/s), it lacked the energy necessary to penetrate even unarmored steel decks or hull plating, although its engine sometimes did so. Fierce fires were caused by the unused gasoline from the aircraft's tanks, but however horrific the casualties which followed, in nature and numbers, in any ship other than a carrier the fire usually caused only superficial damage. More serious damage was inflicted by the *kamikaze*'s bomb, although penetration into the ship was usually limited by the low speed of impact of the aircraft – about one third of that of a free-fall bomb released by a dive-bomber at 3000 feet (900m).

The only suicide raid to get through on 7 January was a JAAF mission which attacked the main amphibious force, the 'Tractor Group,' to the northwest of Mindoro at dusk. *LST.912* was hit but only slightly damaged, with the loss of four men, and the light cruiser *Phoenix* was fortunate when another aircraft, diving straight for her, disintegrated into burning fragments which fell around her. Only four escort carriers were with this group and their fighters were unable to chase away all the Japanese shadowers.

Task Force 38's aircraft, although still hampered by bad weather, made a more positive contribution on the 7th to the protection of the Allied ships in Lingayen Gulf. Harangued before the first launch by Halsey, the pilots 'got down among the weeds' and more than doubled their score of the 6th, claiming to have destroyed 75 aircraft on the ground and four in the air. This day's work effectively broke the back of organized resistance by the Japanese air forces on Luzon, but the cost of this success was high, for 28 aircraft failed to return to the fast carriers.

The Japanese Combined Fleet had meanwhile already accepted the inevitable. On 6 January, after the expenditure of most of the organized *kamikaze* units, the order was given to disband Second Air Fleet and to transfer its surviving elements, personnel and materiel, other than the 30 surviving fighters, to First Air Fleet, with effect from 8 January. Vice-Admiral Ohnishi was to remain in command of First Air Fleet, but would remove his headquarters staff to Formosa, together with his pilots and as many radio technicians as possible. All other personnel would remain on Luzon as ground troops. Vice-Admiral Fukudome flew out to Singapore on 8 January, to take command of the naval forces remaining in the Malaya-East Indies area.

After the relative peace of 7 January, the suicide aircraft appeared in some numbers on the 8th. During the dawn twilight two 'Zeroes,' hotly pursued by Wildcats, attacked the cruiser group and both flew into the side of the *Australia* after first striking the water. One blew a considerable hole above the waterline, but there were no casualties from the attack, other than a Wildcat pilot, who was shot down by mistake by US ships' gunfire. The *Australia* was offered the option of withdrawing but her captain declined and, patched up, she remained with the group.

Half an hour after this attack, it was the turn of the Tractor Group, which had been shadowed almost continuously for 36 hours and was now only 55 miles to the west of Zambales. Several suicide aircraft broke through the CAP, but only two hits were scored, both by JAAF 'Oscars.' The first struck the escort carrier *Kadashan Bay* on the waterline amidships, blowing a large hole in her hull. The shock ruptured her aviation fuel system and heavy flooding caused her to trim five feet by the bows; the small fires were dealt with promptly and there was no loss of life. The damage was too extensive to allow the carrier to continue operations and she therefore transferred as many aircraft as possible to other ships, prior to returning to Leyte. The other suicide aircraft hit the attack transport *Callaway* on the bridge. The crash and consequent gasoline fire killed and injured 43 of the transport's crew but damage was superficial and none of the 1188 US Army troops on board was hurt.

A third major force, the 'Lingayen Attack Force' had met with no opposition during its long passage from the Admiralty Islands, and saw its first action at dusk on the 8th off Cape Bolinao, at the entrance to Lingayen Gulf. Four of the six *kamikazes* were shot down by the CAP, but the other two fenced in the gloom with the slower Wildcats until they saw opportunities for suicide dives on ships. Neither hit, but scored damaging near misses. The first, at 1857, missed the escort carrier *Kitkun Bay*, on her first outing since incurring damage off Samar, sufficiently closely to blow in her side amidships, flooding an engine room and starting a small fire. Counterflooding remedied an initially critical stability problem and she was taken in tow with a 13-degree list. By dawn, she was capable of 10 knots on one engine and joined the escort carrier force, under whose protection her crew carried out first-aid repairs before withdrawal. Less seriously damaged was the Australian landing ship (infantry), HMAS *Westralia*, a converted liner. Her *kamikaze* plunged into the sea under her stern, putting her steering gear out of action temporarily.

The landings took place in the gulf around Lingayen and San Fabian on 9 January. In

ABOVE: *Kamikaze* pilots contemplate a ceremonial banner prior to their mission.

spite of all the activity, with its clear warning of the location and probable timing, the Japanese Army scarcely resisted. The suicide aircraft, though unsuccessful in deterring the amphibious assault, kept coming and continued to inflict damage.

The destroyer escort *Hodges* was clipped by one aircraft which knocked off her foremast and five minutes later, still before dawn, another found the already-damaged *Columbia* boxed in by landing craft and unable to take avoiding action. The cruiser was hit on the bridge and the instantaneous explosion of the bomb blew the forward gunnery director overboard, beside inflicting serious splinter casualties – 24 men were killed and 68 injured. There was then a lull until 1302, when four 'Vals,' escorted by four fighters, approached. Two were shot down by CAP but the others hit the battleship *Mississippi* and the long-suffering *Australia*. The first slid along the port edge of the battleship's upper deck, killing 23 and injuring 63 members of her guns' crews, and then over the side, where its bomb finally exploded. Damage to the big ship from a small ammunition fire and underwater shock, was negligible. The *Australia's* attacker misjudged his run at her bridge and hit the cruiser's foremast, which swung the 'Val' through the fore funnel. There were no casualties, but the ship had now suffered more than enough cumulative damage to earn her release from the operation.

The *kamikazes* returned at dusk and attacked for over an hour. After an early near miss on the destroyer *Bush*, they did not even come close to their targets. But the *Colorado* did not escape unhurt, for a stray AA shell hit her in the superstructure and, among other casualties, killed her radar fighter-direction team. She remained in the gulf, but the damaged cruisers *Louisville*, *Columbia* and HMAS *Australia* and the escort carrier *Kadashan Bay* left with the first return convoy which departed after dark.

The night of 9/10 January was enlivened by the appearance of 'suicide boats,' 18-foot motor boats powered by truck engines and capable of up to 25 knots. Intended for attacks on ships at anchor, and built in large numbers, these army craft carried a single 440-pound depth-charge which was released alongside the target. Navy *Shinyo* suicide boats were equipped with contact explosive charges or, later, simple rockets which were made by screwing a motor to a 104lb (47kg) short-caliber eight-inch (203mm) naval shell. This first use, by the Japanese Army, achieved surprise and some measure of success, for the destroyer *Eaton*, the attack transport *Warhawk* and *LST.610* were damaged, a couple of landing craft (infantry) sunk and three others seriously damaged. The most effective counter to these nuisances was to get under way, but this was not always possible and anchorage defense depended upon the vigilance of lookouts, backed up by immediately available 40mm and 20mm gunfire. Equally important was close control of

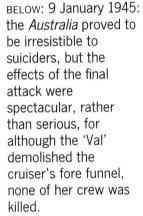

BELOW: 9 January 1945: the *Australia* proved to be irresistible to suiciders, but the effects of the final attack were spectacular, rather than serious, for although the 'Val' demolished the cruiser's fore funnel, none of her crew was killed.

friendly boat traffic within the anchorage.

The 10th began and ended with successful suicide attacks. Before dawn, the destroyer *Dashiell* was missed shortly before a twin-engined aircraft hit the destroyer escort *Leray Wilson*, on anti-submarine patrol outside the gulf. Apart from a badly damaged funnel and jammed torpedo tubes, the DE escaped lightly, with only eight men killed and five injured. Within the gulf, life was quiet and unloading went ahead quickly enough for two convoys, of empty transports and landing craft, to leave at dusk. An hour later, a JAAF 'Nick' made a head-on attack on the departing transport *DuPage*, hitting her on the port side of the bridge and sliding aft down the superstructure. The plane's fuel burned fiercely and 32 men were killed and 157 injured but the ship remained with the convoy. The *Kitkun Bay* joined and provided CAP on the following day.

No Japanese aircraft appeared on 11 January, but sufficient were scraped together during the day to launch what amounted to a major effort on the 12th. At 0700, the DE *Gilligan* was hit by a 'Betty' bomber which demolished her after superstructure and caused fierce fires. Half an hour later, her sister-ship *Richard W Suesens*, covering her while an APD assisted with firefighting, was missed by a *kamikaze* which passed over her low enough to cut radio wire aerials. Several unsuccessful attacks were made lower down the gulf but the 'All Clear' was finally given at 0745. Eight minutes later, four 'Nicks' got in by trailing a friendly flying boat. Two missed their targets, the APD *Belknap* shot down a third but could not avoid the fourth, whose bombs exploded on impact amidships, killing 38 men and damaging the old destroyer beyond repair. Fifteen minutes after that attack, three 'Zeroes,' pursued by the CAP, attacked a small slow outbound convoy, near-missing *LST.700*, which was slightly

damaged, and an attack transport, which was not.

An inbound supply convoy was picked up by the Japanese as it passed to the west of Manila Bay and it was subjected to JAAF suicide attacks at shortly after noon and at dusk. As was typical with the army suicide pilots, the largest transports were targeted. On the first occasion, there was no warning before an aircraft flew into the side of the Liberty ship SS *Otis Skinner*, the fuselage continued into the hull, where a bomb exploded, starting a fire. Although badly damaged, the *Otis Skinner* suffered no loss of life and continued to Lingayen. The later attack was made in greater strength and three Liberty ships were damaged, the DD *Field* and EN *Westcott* superficially by near misses, but the *Kyle V Johnson* very severely, with the loss of 129 men killed, by an aircraft which started extensive fires on her upper deck. *LST.778* was undamaged by two near misses but did not escape unhurt, for she and *LST.710* were victims of misdirected 'friendly' AA gunfire.

The final 'honors' went to the JAAF, whose pilots damaged three widely-separated ships in a 48-minute period between 0810 and 0858 on 13 January. The first attack, 60 miles to the west of Manila Bay, scored a direct hit on *LST.700*, attacked 24 hours earlier by the final JNAF attempt. This time, the LST was left dead in the water with her engine room flooded and had to be towed to Mindoro. Eleven minutes later and about 40 miles to the north, the attack transport *Zeilin*, with a fast outbound convoy, was hit on her after cargo hatches and moderately damaged by the impact and resulting fire.

The Lingayen campaign ended as it had begun, with a JAAF fighter flying into an escort carrier. The victim was the *Salamaua*, operating some 40 miles northwest of Lingayen Gulf. Late warning of the raid prevented effective use of the CAP and several

LEFT: A captured Japanese 'Maru-Ni' suicide boat under test. Powered by an 80bhp gasoline engine, the 18-foot craft could attain up to 28 knots while carrying a 440-pound depth-charge on the rack behind the driver.

ABOVE: A large number of crewmen watch as a suicide aircraft is shot down about 200 yards astern of an escort carrier at Lingayen. Had the aircraft reached the ship few of the spectators would have survived!

BELOW: Pre-dawn briefing for another Special Attack unit (there appears to be some difference of opinion as to the location of the target).

aircraft broke through to be shot down by AA fire or miss completely. The successful fighter-bomber, possibly a Nakajima 'Frank,' carrying two 550lb bombs, struck the carrier's flight deck abaft of amidships and its engine and fuselage went through all the decks, coming to rest on top of the double-bottom fuel tanks. The bombs took separate paths, one leaving the ship at the waterline without exploding, but causing the after engine room to flood, while the other detonated low down, badly damaging the starboard machinery spaces and steering gear. A moderate hangar fire was quickly extinguished and fatal casualties were remarkably light, with only 15 men dead. The *Salamaua* was left dead in the water, with no power and an eight-degree list, but with some outside assistance her

crew were able to patch up her machinery and she left with a Leyte-bound convoy that evening.

The US Army's return to Luzon had been a bloody affair for the men of the Allied navies and the US Merchant Marine, who had lost 697 men killed and over 1300 injured by suicide attack and another 74 dead in conventional air attacks. The latter stages of the Mindoro operation had shown that the Japanese pilots, and particularly those of the Imperial Japanese Army, were becoming more accurate. They were becoming adept at penetrating strong, alert defenses and the hitting rate on 5 and 6 January was never to be exceeded. But they were still unable to sink ships – the only outright Allied loss caused by a single suicide aircraft had been the very first, the carrier *Ommaney Bay*. Of the other 29 ships which took direct hits, only one subsequently sank and two others were damaged beyond repair. Three escort carriers were forced to withdraw due to damage to their machinery, but amphibious shipping and Liberty ships forced on to complete their tasks despite damage, while the battered cruisers of the bombardment force remained on station despite repeated hits. Of the *Australia*'s experience, Admiral Fraser signaled to the Admiralty: 'It is doubtful whether five hits by any other comparable weapon would have caused so little fundamental damage.'

The Japanese Navy remained unaware of the fundamental weakness of what was now its primary weapon. From his new base on Formosa, Vice-Admiral Ohnishi set about building a new *kamikaze* corps. Morison states that 47 JNAF aircraft escaped to Formosa and Inoguchi that about 100 reinforcements were received from Japan and from these was formed, on 18 January 1945, the first organized Formosa-based *kamikaze* force, the 'Zeroes' and 'Judies' of the '*Niitaka* Unit.' Ohnishi was present to exhort his volunteers: 'Even if we are defeated, the noble spirit of this *kamikaze* attack corps will keep our homeland from ruin. Without this spirit, ruin would certainly follow defeat.' Fine words for the seventeenth-century samurai, but insanity in the mouth of the leader of a highly technical, twentieth-century fighting force. *Bushido* ultimately damaged the nation which it was supposed to represent, for Ohnishi and his like condemned to unnecessary deaths the brightest and best of their generation. While their sacrifice was to inflict damage and loss of ships and life, it had no effect on Allied strategy or determination – the sole criteria of success in total war.

FOR the first time in a year of operations, the Fast Carrier Task Force had failed in a primary mission, due in large part initially to bad weather but later to lack of persistence. Admiral Halsey had long dreamed of a raiding cruise into the South China Sea, to strike at the untouched Japanese-controlled bases on the coasts of China and Indochina, and during the first week of January 1945, he justified this plan to Admiral Nimitz on the basis that major Japanese naval units based in the area posed a threat to the Mindoro-Lingayen shipping. The fact was that nothing larger than a training cruiser was located between Formosa and Saigon, or closer than Singapore. What could not be known was that Combined Fleet had no intention of using the two old battleships and such cruisers as were serviceable at Singapore in defense of Luzon, which had, effec-

third visit to Formosa. During the forenoon, when good weather was experienced for the first time, the strikes concentrated on shipping and not until the afternoon were the airfields properly covered. The wisdom of this order of priorities must be doubted, for it gave the newly-formed *Niitaka* unit a chance to strike. In all, six 'Judies' and two 'Zeroes,' escorted by seven fighters, took off, but it is evident from the US action report that this was but one of at least four formations which approached between 1206 and 1250.

The first raid attacked TG 38.1, 90 miles off the southeastern coast of Formosa. One aircraft broke through the CAP, bombed the light carrier *Langley* and rendered her unable to operate aircraft for three hours. Two minutes later, four *kamikazes* attacked TG 58.3, 24 miles to the north of TG 38.1,

CHAPTER 4

FAST CARRIER ENCOUNTERS

LEFT: 1210, 21 January 1945: smoke from burning aircraft in *Ticonderoga*'s hangar pours from the impact point of the bomb which the *kamikaze* released before itself hitting near the forward elevator. One of the 245 casualties lies at bottom left.

tively, been abandoned. Halsey, too, abandoned the offensive Allied operation against Luzon.

Task Force 38 resumed strikes on 9 January after refueling, but instead of blanketing the Luzon airfields, whose suicide aircraft were still inflicting damage in and around Lingayen Gulf, Admiral McCain sent over 700 sorties against Formosa and the Sakishima Islands, where they destroyed less than 50 aircraft, many of them dummies. These operations covered the passage into the South China Sea of the fast carriers and their supporting replenishment group. Bad weather permitted strikes on only three of the 10 days spent between the Philippines and China, but 50 merchant vessels, naval auxiliaries and minor warships were sunk and over 150 aircraft destroyed for the loss of 82 carrier aircraft, many of them caused by the weather.

On 21 January, TF 38 began the final phase of this series of operations with a

and one which got through crashed into the *Ticonderoga*'s crowded after deck park, setting fire to the aircraft; the bomb went through the flight deck and exploded in the hangar, causing fires which spread down a further three decks. Another raid appeared from the south (giving rise to the suspicion that it had come from Luzon) and was dealt with by the *Cowpens*' CAP before it could close TG 38.1.

The next wave, of eight *kamikazes* and five escorts, lost six suicide aircraft to the CAP but the survivors pressed on into the AA gunfire, which accounted for a seventh. The temporary survivor flew into the still-blazing *Ticonderoga*'s island at 1250, engulfing the superstructure in a gasoline fire which spread to the aircraft in the carrier's forward deck park, hitherto untouched. The fires were not brought under control for another hour and a half, by which time the flooding caused by firefighting had given the ship a nine-degree list. Thirty-six air-

craft were written off in the fires and there were 345 casualties, 143 of them fatal.

There had meanwhile been another casualty. The destroyer *Maddox* was on 'Tomcat' picket duty halfway to Formosa and neither she nor the 'delousing' CAP managed to pick up a lone *kamikaze* which followed a returning strike. The 'Zero' took the opportunity for a deliberate attack but, although he hit the destroyer's bridge, his aircraft bounced off into the sea, where the bomb exploded, causing extensive above-water blast and splinter damage (which killed seven men and injured 32) and under-water shock damage. The *Ticonderoga* and *Maddox* withdrew at nightfall with an escort to return to Ulithi.

The rest of Task Force 38 followed 24 hours later, after a day of unopposed strikes on northern Formosa and the Ryukyu Islands. At midnight on 26/27 January, Halsey handed over command of the Third Fleet to Admiral Raymond Spruance, under whom the same units became the Fifth Fleet. During this last month at sea, Halsey and his carrier commander (McCain) had achieved little of note apart from the South China Sea anti-shipping successes and at unprecedented cost – the period had cost the fast carriers 201 of their aircraft and 167 aircrew, over and above more than 200 men lost aboard ships. Vice-Admiral Marc

ABOVE: President Roosevelt with his two Pacific theater Commanders-in-Chief, General Douglas MacArthur (left) and Admiral Chester Nimitz.

ABOVE RIGHT: 21 January 1945: *Ticonderoga*, off Formosa, is near-missed shortly before the first of two *kamikazes* hits which were to put her out of action for several months.

RIGHT: 1210, 21 January 1945: seen from the light cruiser *Miami*, *Ticonderoga*'s hangar burns after the first of two *kamikaze* hits off Formosa.

LEFT: Marc A Mitscher, one of the most capable and inspiring air commanders of WWII.

Mitscher resumed tactical command of the carriers. His return was universally welcomed by those whom he was to lead.

Although the exact details had yet to be worked out, Royal Navy fast carriers were about to begin operations in the Pacific. They left their Indian Ocean base in Ceylon on 16 January 1945 for Australia and struck at Japanese-controlled oil refineries at Palembang, Sumatra, on 24 and 29 January. Apart from the outstanding success they enjoyed against these economically strategic targets, the operation was marked by the first suicide attack on the British Pacific Fleet (BPF).

The Royal Navy had been kept fully informed of this latest development and had modified US Navy tactics to suit its own air defense organization, with its differing strengths and weaknesses. The major weakness was in lack of numbers of aircraft: in January 1945, two 'standard' air group complements were embarked in the US Navy's Essex-class carriers – either 54 fighters and 42 torpedo-bombers and dive-bombers, or 73 fighters and 30 attack air-

craft. The biggest of the four British carriers had only 40 single-seat fighters, a dozen two-seat reconnaissance-fighters (Fairey Fireflies) and 21 torpedo-bombers. Altogether, the fighter strength of the fleet totaled 143 aircraft of three types – Supermarine Seafires, Vought Corsairs and, least numerous, the Grumman Hellcat.

The reason for the smaller aircraft complements, on a similar ship tonnage, was that the British fleet carriers had armored flight decks and hangar sides, whereas the US Navy had no armor above the hangar deck. The three-inch (76mm) protection had proved to be adequate against 500lb bombs in the Mediterranean and was expected to be able to keep out *kamikazes*.

On 29 January 1945, seven Kawasaki 'Lily' light bombers of the JAAF's '*Shichisi Mitate* Special Corps' counterattacked the BPF at low level as its own strikes were returning from Palembang. The radar picture was confused by the presence of over 100 friendly aircraft and the first two of three Seafire CAP interceptions did not occur until just before the 'Lilies' entered the gun

BELOW: The four carriers of the British Pacific Fleet, operating as TF.57, leave Ulithi for their first operation in the Pacific in March 1945. At that time the force included *Indomitable, Victorious, Illustrious* and *Indefatigable*.

ABOVE: Japanese Army suicide pilots receive their orders at an airfield on Kyushu in the spring of 1945.

defense zone. The last pair of Seafires chased the five remaining bombers inside the screen and, with the help of a returning Corsair and a Hellcat which had just been scrambled, splashed all of them between the lines of ships and among the intense automatic AA fire. One Seafire was slightly damaged and the Hellcat was written off by the gunfire, but the only ship to be damaged was the carrier HMS *Illustrious*, hit by a heavy AA shell. This affair, minor by Pacific standards, gave the BPF useful experience and confidence (not entirely misplaced) in its ability to deal with suicide attacks.

The Japanese Naval Air Force enjoyed a four-week break from anti-shipping operations after the last carrier strikes on Formosa on 21 January. First Air Fleet was built up to a strength of about 150 operational aircraft but it was no longer the main frontline force. The Japanese Home Islands were now open to direct attack and priority went to the Fifth Air Fleet on Kyushu, and the Third Air Fleet based around Tokyo, which mustered 550 aircraft between them. In reserve were the training units of Tenth Air Fleet with 900 aircraft. All three home-based air fleets were reorganizing to train *kamikaze* units.

In spite of the heavy losses of 1944, production had kept ahead of wastage and the JNAF was to have more fighters and attack aircraft of more advanced models on hand on 1 April 1945 than it possessed a year earlier. What was lacking was an adequate pool of pilots. The fuel shortage which had

become serious from mid-1944 was now acute and with the oil supply from the Netherlands East Indies virtually cut off by the loss of the Philippines, no improvement could be foreseen. In order to train sufficient pilots, the training syllabus was cut to 100 hours – once in a unit, the inexperienced pilot could expect no more than 15 flying hours a month to learn his operational job and keep his hand in. The latter was important, for some of the new types – the Kawanishi 'Frances' attack aircraft and 'George' fighter, for example – were not as straightforward and forgiving as the 'Betty' and 'Zero,' and required considerable practice to fly to their best tactical advantage.

The US fast carriers finally attacked Japan itself on 16 and 17 February 1945. Four of the nine Essex class ships now had US Marine Corps Corsairs embarked and all had sacrificed torpedo and dive-bombers to increase their fighter strength to 70 per ship. Damage had reduced the number of light carriers to five, but the night carriers (*Enterprise* and *Saratoga*) were both large ships. Despite bad weather, over 500 Japanese aircraft were claimed as destroyed in the air and on the ground during the two days. The figure was probably at least double the actual score and US Navy losses were themselves heavy: 88 carrier aircraft lost to the enemy and the weather. No JNAF aircraft got close to the carriers, thanks mainly to the effectiveness of the 'delousing' routine and the 'Tomcat' CAPs.

The strikes were the overture to the invasion of Iwo Jima, a small volcanic island in the Bonins group, 660 miles south of Tokyo. The main objective of the seizure of this island was to establish a forward airfield to support the Boeing B-29 strategic bomber offensive against Japan, providing a base for escort fighters and emergency facilities for the Superfortresses themselves. The Japanese had correctly assessed that Iwo Jima would be the next target but did not plan any major operations for its defense – the garrison would be supported only by a limited conventional bombing and *kamikaze* effort.

D-Day for Iwo Jima was 19 February 1945, after three days of softening up by naval gunfire and aircraft from 10 escort carriers. The first Japanese air attack was delivered on the night of the 18/19th, a medium-level raid which scored hits on a DMS and an APD and forced them to withdraw. There were no attacks during daylight on D-Day,

and although the fast carriers were teased by a formation after dark, only two aircraft approached and were shot down by AA fire. Bad weather kept the JNAF away for the next two days but in the late afternoon of 21 February it cleared sufficiently for Vice-Admiral Kimpei Teraoka's Third Air Fleet to commit two dozen *kamikazes*, backed up by shadowers to cooperate in the attacks.

At 1628, the night carrier *Saratoga* was operating independently about 35 miles to the northwest of Iwo Jima, covering the amphibious shipping when she vectored a CAP toward an inbound formation which other ships had evaluated as friendly. Two 'friendly' 'Zeroes' were shot down at 1650 but at least six others escaped into the low cloud and the 'Sara' began scrambling every available Hellcat. The fifteenth fighter had just left the catapult when, at 1700, the *kamikazes* arrived. The first four 'Zeroes' hit the carrier, two bouncing off the water into her starboard side, one diving into the flight deck forward and the fourth hitting the large crane; the other two were shot down close to the carrier. Three bombs went off inside the hull, causing severe blast damage and starting fires on the hangar deck to add to those blazing on the flight deck.

Twenty minutes later, a small number of *kamikazes* began attacks on groups of ships in a holding position about 50 miles to the southeast of Iwo Jima. Three scored hits: a 'Jill' on the net-layer *Keokuk*, and unidentified aircraft on *LSTs.477* and *.809*. The *Keokuk* caught fire but neither of the LSTs was seriously damaged.

The next raids arrived simultaneously at 1845 in the vicinities of the *Saratoga*, whose internal fires had been brought under control minutes before, and the *Keokuk*, which was still burning. Both strikes were skillfully coordinated, that on the carrier being illuminated by flares, while the other, 75 miles off to the southeast, was a well-timed combined *kamikaze* and torpedo attack. The *Saratoga* and her screen shot down four out of five aircraft which attacked her, but the last got through unobserved and hit the forward flight deck at a shallow angle. The bomb, believed to be a 1100-pounder detonated on impact, blowing a large hole in the flight deck, but the aircraft itself slid over the side. The *Saratoga* survived, though she had lost 123 men and 36 aircraft, and would be out of action for three months.

The other raid resisted the lure of the burning net-layer and found the escort carrier group. Of four torpedo-bombers which went for the *Lunga Point*, one 'Jill' was shot down before the dropping point and another

afterward; the three torpedoes all missed very narrowly, but one of the attackers, on fire, turned from evasion to a suicide dive, clipped the carrier's island with its wing-tip and skidded across the flight deck, leaving minor fires in its wake before it crashed into the sea. The last escaped. Simultaneously, two *kamikazes* attacked the *Bismarck Sea*. One was shot down but the other crashed into the side of the after end of the hangar, setting fire to aircraft. Two minutes later, as this fire was being brought under control, a third *kamikaze* dived into and through the flight deck in the same section of the ship, the explosion of its bomb and gasoline starting uncontrollable fires among aircraft on the flight and hangar decks. At 1902 the torpedo warheads in the hangar stowage 'cooked off,' blowing out the after end of the hangar and wrecking the ship's stern. The *Bismarck Sea* was abandoned and her 725 survivors (out of 943 men) were picked up by ships of the screen. The carrier burned for three hours before flooding caused her to capsize and sink. She was the third and last escort carrier to be sunk by suicide attack.

Only 24 *kamikazes* had been involved in these, the only suicide attacks of the Iwo Jima campaign. It was Third Air Fleet's first essay and the pilots had shown a high level of skill, for 10 of them had scored hits on five ships and an eleventh had narrowly missed inflicting heavy damage on a sixth – the *Lunga Point* – in an impromptu suicide attack. But the US Navy's personnel losses on this night, though heavy (358 dead and missing, and over 300 injured), were insignificant compared with the casualties being suffered by the US Marines ashore on Iwo Jima, where 5900 men died and 17,270 were wounded in overcoming a garrison of 23,500 Japanese.

Task Force 58, less the night-flying Task Group 58.5, returned to Ulithi on 4 March 1945 to replenish and rest. One Essex class and one light carrier withdrew for refit, their places being taken by two Essexes – the *Franklin* and *Intrepid*, newly repaired after *kamikaze* damage – and a light carrier. Ulithi, some 1200 miles southeast of Okinawa, had long been a 'safe' forward base. Although other islands in the Western Carolines group were still occupied by the Japanese, they were incapable of offensive action against a base whose defenses included day and night-fighter units. It therefore came as a complete surprise when, at 1915 on 11 March, a twin-engined aircraft appeared out of the night and flew into the after end of the fully-lit fast carrier *Randolph*.

The aircraft was a 'Frances' of Vice-

BELOW: The JNAF's Kawanishi 'Emily' flying-boat was used for long-range scouting but despite a heavy defensive armament suffered very heavy losses to carrier fighters and even (as in the incident pictured) to long-range patrol aircraft.

Admiral Matome Ugaki's Fifth Air Fleet. With 23 others it had taken off from southern Kyushu and, led by four Kawanishi 'Emily' flying-boats, had flown around 1400 miles in poor weather and against a strong head-wind to reach the Carolines. Thirteen of the bombers fell out during the 10-hour flight and minor navigational errors delayed the arrival of the survivors until after dark. Only the one hit was scored, the 1760-pound bomb carried putting the *Randolph* out of action for a month. During the next 25 minutes, the other 'Frances' all either flew into islands which they mistook for ships or missed the real thing.

Nine Essexes, five light and one night carrier left Ulithi on 14 March to attack the Japanese Home Islands once again, this time as a precursor to the invasion of Okinawa. Strikes on 18 March were directed at 45 airfields on Kyushu, Shikoku and western Honshu, where units of Fifth Air Fleet and of the JAAF were based. The arrival of the carrier aircraft was not unexpected, for reconnaissance aircraft had picked up Task Force 58 during the afternoon of 17 March and shadowers had kept in touch throughout the night. The fighter sweeps therefore found relatively few Japanese aircraft airborne or on the ground – they were either well dispersed or already airborne to counterattack.

Task Group 58.4, 75 miles to the south of Shikoku, attracted most of the attention from conventional bombers and *kamikazes*, two raids managing to get through the CAP to damage three large carriers. Only the *Intrepid* came under *kamikaze* attack, suffering a minor hangar fire when blazing fragments from a shot-down 'Betty' struck her. The *Yorktown* and *Enterprise* were slightly damaged by dive-bombers. Over 50 Japanese aircraft were shot down by CAP and gunfire.

Fifth Air Fleet returned early on the 19th, after the American carriers had launched strikes to attack the Japanese Fleet laid up at Kure. Within two minutes of one another, two large carriers, in different task groups, were hit and put out of action by dive-bombers: the *Franklin* was all but given up for lost as fires swept the ship and she came to a dead stop, and the *Wasp* suffered fire damage to her hangar and flight deck that kept her out of action for three months. As she fought her fires, a *kamikaze* clipped her deck-edge lift before crashing into the sea. Nine hundred and twenty-five men died and over 500 were injured in the two carriers.

The *Franklin* was towed slowly out of the

LEFT: 19 March 1945: conventional dive-bombing inflicted the most severe damage to be survived by any aircraft carrier: the *Franklin*'s fires burned for over five hours and killed 724 of her crew.

area until noon on 20 March, when she was able to make 15 knots under her own power. Three hours later her group came under attack again. The CAP shot down seven aircraft, AA fire accounted for another seven, but one 'Zero' got through to dive on the *Hancock*, which was refueling a destroyer, the *Halsey Powell*. The *kamikaze* missed the carrier but not the destroyer, hitting her on the quarter-deck and killing 10 men. The small bomb went out through the bottom of the ship, as did the 'Zero's' engine, causing severe flooding and a steering-gear breakdown which resulted in near-collision with the carrier. TF 58's withdrawal was now slowed by the limping *Halsey Powell*. During the remaining hours of daylight, small numbers of JNAF aircraft attacked, but the most serious damage suffered was inflicted by 'friendly' AA fire, which put the only night carrier's flight deck out of action overnight.

The intensive Japanese reconnaissance activity on 20 March led to one of the strangest suicide attacks of the entire campaign. The US submarine *Devilfish* was on the surface northwest of the Bonin Islands, and 300 miles south of TF 58, heading for her patrol area off Japan when an aircraft was sighted at short range. The submarine dived quickly, but her conning tower was just going under when the aircraft struck her, wrecking the periscope standards superstructure. Blinded, but with her hull and engines intact, the *Devilfish* had to abandon

LEFT: Kanoya airfield, March 1945: 'Betty' aircrew, sitting near their 'Ohka'-laden bombers, await the order to take off.

RIGHT: 21 March 1945: *Hornet*'s Hellcat pilots record the destruction of two of the 18 'Betty'-'Ohka' combinations destroyed in a few minutes to the southeast of Kyushu.

her patrol and return to base, the victim of an opportunity attack.

Admiral Ugaki played his ace on 21 March. The 'Ohka' manned glider bombs and 'Betty' mother-planes of the 721st Air Group had been under his command since 10 February, but they had been held back until a really worthwhile target presented itself. A report from a shadower that one US carrier task group, 320 miles out from Kyushu, appeared to have no fighter protection triggered the decision to use the new weapon against a valuable but temporarily 'soft' target. Eighteen 'Betties,' each carrying an 'Ohka,' took off from Toizaki at about midday, escorted by 30 fighters.

Had the piloted bomb's debut been coordinated with the mixed conventional and *kamikaze* attacks that had been employed during the preceding two days, it would have stood a realistic chance of success. With the CAPs fully committed at all heights, the escorted 'Betty' formation might have reached a release point in sufficient numbers to make a victory possible. As it happened, the large but solitary formation was detected by radar at a range of over 100 miles distance and, undistracted by other raids, all four task groups launched extra fighters until over 150 Hellcats and Corsairs were airborne. It fell to 24 fighters from TG 58.1 to make the interception, over 50 miles out from the nearest US ship. While the *Bennington*'s Corsairs held off the 'Zero' escort, shooting down over 20 of the Japanese fighters, Hellcats from the *Hornet* and *Belleau Wood* dealt with the 'Betties' – all of them.

Fifth Air Flotilla had sent 193 aircraft against Task Force 58 on the three days and only 32 returned to their bases. As many as 350 more, JAAF and JNAF, had been destroyed on the airfields. On the eve of the Okinawa invasion, the main Japanese counterattack forces had thus been seriously weakened and would have to draw on the other air fleets and air armies for replacement aircraft and, as they became available, pilots. The conventional dive-bombers had, however, scored a notable success in forcing the withdrawal of an entire carrier task group – TG 58.2, two badly damaged Essexes and the less badly damaged *Enterprise* protecting them. The 116 US Navy aircraft lost in combat could readily be replaced from the reserve stock held at sea in the replenishment escort carriers, but the withdrawal of TG 58.2's 176 fighters and 80 attack aircraft, including the specialized night-fighter and strike force aboard the *Enterprise*, was a serious weakening at a critical juncture.

THE island of Okinawa, the largest of the Ryukyu chain which stretches between Japan and Formosa, was essential to what remained of the outer defenses of Japan, as an outpost of both Kyushu and the northeast coast of China, and a stepping stone to Formosa. American occupation would effectively cut off Formosa from supply by the most direct route and threaten the Japanese line of communication with mainland China, one of its few remaining sources of raw materials. For the US forces, possession would provide airfields within 350 miles of Japan itself and excellent anchorages for mounting the invasion of the Home Islands.

The Combined Fleet was given command of all air forces (including the JAAF's Sixth Air Army) allocated to the defense of Okinawa, with Vice-Admiral Ugaki in day-to-

working in the approaches to Kerama. Landings on the latter took place on the 26th and the group was secured by the 28th. Base facilities were already moving in and the anchorage was rapidly developed to support the main invasion.

Suicide attacks did not begin until 26 March, when Combined Fleet ordered Ten-Go to be executed. Fifth Air Fleet, mauled during the previous week, could not mount a major effort until replacements and reinforcements had been received from Third Air Fleet; Sixth Air Army was ordered to attack the transports off Kerama but it too was regrouping and unable to comply. The JNAF was thus able to dispatch only small formations of *kamikaze* and conventional bombers to harass American operations during the opening phase. The full defen-

CHAPTER 5

OKINAWA – THE FINAL BATTLE

day tactical command. The plan for the defense of Okinawa – Operation Ten-Go – originally ordered Fifth Air Fleet to give priority to the amphibious shipping, but Ugaki, fearing that his *kamikaze* units would be wiped out on the ground while waiting for the landing force's arrival, managed to convince the staff that he should be given more discretion in targeting. The fast carriers would be given equal priority but, as had been seen in the previous campaigns, individual pilots, inexperienced or *in extremis*, would attack targets of lesser immediate value, diluting the weight of the offensive.

The initial form of the invasion took the Japanese by surprise, for instead of landing on Okinawa, an infantry division seized a group of offshore islands, the Kerama Retto, 15 miles to the southwest. The operation began on 24 March, with TF 58 striking at airfields and suicide boat bases on Okinawa and neighboring islands and minesweepers

sive organization was not yet in place and these early raids slipped through to damage 13 ships off Kerama and another in the only attack on the fast carriers. All but three of these were destroyer types (which included DMS and APDs) and only three sustained damage which obliged them to retire for repairs (the destroyers *Kimberley* and *O'Brien* and the DMS *Dorsey*). That left 62 destroyers and a dozen DMSs.

After a pause on 28 March, the suicide aircraft arrived before dawn on the next day. About two dozen were involved and most got past the CAP to attack the Kerama anchorage, but the intense AA fire destroyed 13 aircraft and only one direct hit was scored, on a support craft – *LSM(R).188* which was badly damaged.

The full elaborate defensive organization came into operation on 29 March. Already on station were the two fast carrier task forces, TF 58 to the north and east to interdict airfields on Kyushu and provide CAP

between Japan and Okinawa, and the British carriers to the southwest, interdicting the Sakishima Island group and guarding against the intervention of the relatively weak First Air Fleet based on Formosa. The outer ring of the inner defenses was a screen of 15 radar picket stations, at distances between 74 and 35 miles away from the southwest corner of Okinawa. Eight stations were occupied by pairs of destroyers, 19 of which had embarked specially-trained fighter-direction teams to control their own CAPs, which were provided by the US fast carriers and the escort carriers, later assisted by shore-based US Marine Corps fighters. Over Kerama and the groups inshore off Okinawa, escort carriers provided CAPs controlled by teams in six of the amphibious headquarters ships and most of the 10 battleships; there was also a radar station operational ashore on one of the Kerama group and a second opened on 1 April, when the main landings began on Okinawa. Strong though these layered defenses were, the potential for confusion was high and a major weakness was the lack of sufficient night-fighters.

A small dawn *kamikaze* raid on 31 March inflicted what could have been a very serious loss on the US Fifth Fleet. Two aircraft were shot down but the third hit the fleet flagship, the cruiser *Indianapolis*, causing severe damage. Casualties were relatively light and did not include Admiral Spruance, who moved with his staff to a battleship, where he was again to come under attack later in the operation.

The first hit on a fast carrier was scored before the troops touched down on Okinawa on 1 April. The target was HMS *Indefatigable*, whose CAP destroyed three 'Zeroes' attacking from Formosa but failed to stop a fourth which piled up on the three-inch armor at the base of her island. Off the invasion beaches on Okinawa, the first hits were scored on amphibious shipping (two transports and two LSTs) in small-scale dawn and dusk raids, which also damaged the battleship *West Virginia* and put the DMS *Adams* out of action for months. Raids continued to come in during the night, several being broken up by the night-fighter Hellcat CAPs controlled by the picket destroyers. One group got through to Kerama at about 0300 and hit two freighters and a support landing craft. The 2nd proved to be the transports' worst day of the operation for, as well as the night *kamikaze* raid, the JAAF's first major effort, at dusk, found a transport convoy and hit four more freighters and the APD *Dickerson*. Towed to Kerama, the last was found to be damaged beyond repair

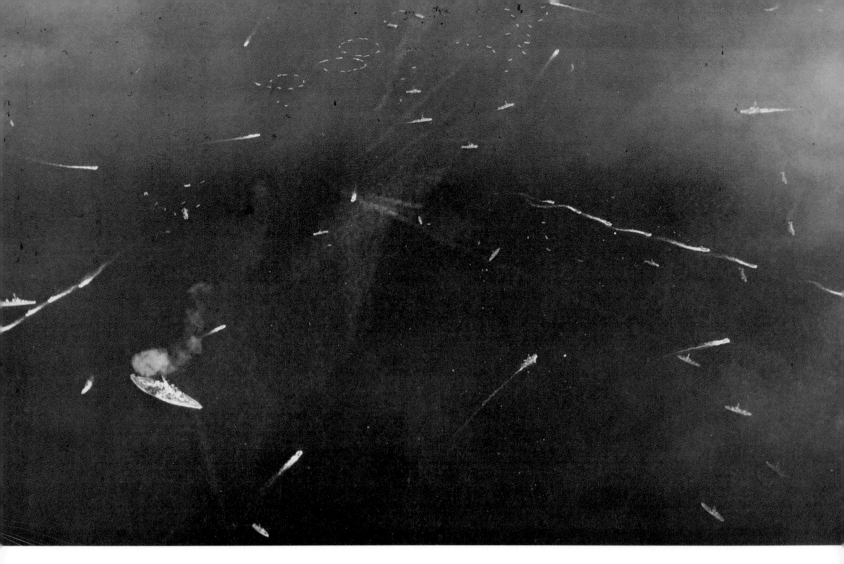

and she was scuttled two days later, the first ship to be lost to suicide attack during Operation Iceberg.

The escort carrier support group escaped attack until the late afternoon of 3 April, when a pair of 'Zeroes' appeared without warning and near-missed the *Wake Island*. The explosion of one bomb caused some flooding but shock damage to the machinery was sufficient to oblige the carrier to withdraw to Guam. Inshore, *LCI.82* was hit by a *Shinyo* suicide boat and sank during the night of 3/4 April, and *LST.599* was damaged beyond repair by a *kamikaze* which managed to get past the otherwise efficient pickets.

By 5 April, Admiral Ugaki was ready to launch the full weight of his JNAF and JAAF suicide and conventional forces against the invaders. Just under 700 aircraft, of which 230 were *kamikazes* and 125 were in army suicide units, had been gathered for the first *Kikusui* operation, which was launched on 6 April. No use was made of 'Ohka' glider bombs, although with saturation raids planned it would seem to have been an ideal opportunity.

The main attack began in mid-afternoon, with reconnaissance aircraft dropping 'window' (radar-reflective foil) to draw off the CAPs. Task Force 58's fighters were not to

be diverted and claimed to have slaughtered 250 Japanese aircraft before they reached the destroyer picket screen and 136 over Okinawa; another 55 were shot down by the escort carriers' Wildcats and 35 by AA gunfire. Twenty-two separate raids, with an estimated 180-plus suicide aircraft, managed to deliver attacks in the Okinawa area, according to the US Navy's analysts. Concentrated into a short span of time, the four hours between 1500 and 1900, it was not surprising that such numbers resulted in the greatest tally of hits and damaging near misses (at least 41) scored in a single day. Of the 24 ships which suffered, however, only four could be regarded as high-value targets – two merchant ships (*Hobbs Victory* and *Logan Victory*) carrying ammunition and *LST.447*, all of which were lost, and the carrier *Illustrious*, which sustained extensive underwater damage of which she remained quite unaware. One raid went for Task Group 58.1 but scored only one hit, on the destroyer *Haynsworth* which had to withdraw. The light carrier *San Jacinto* and another destroyer were peppered by splinters, while three other *kamikazes* missed well wide.

Picket Station 1, some 50 miles to the north of Kerama, proved to be a 'honey pot' for the *kamikazes*. The destroyers *Bush* and

Colhoun were sunk outright by seven hits between them and the support landing craft *LCS(L).64* damaged, but they absorbed the efforts of about 40 'Zeroes' and 'Vals' which might have found more profitable targets nearer to Okinawa. But even that is doubtful, for 35 JNAF suicide aircraft picked on a minesweeping group and a nearby destroyer: the destroyer *Howorth* survived one hit and two near misses, as did the modern DMS *Rodman*, although she was hit three times, and it took five direct hits to reduce her sister-ship, the DMS *Emmons*, to the state where she had to be scuttled. Three smaller minesweepers were also damaged. Elsewhere inshore, four 'Jills' out of 12 in a raid which ignored nearby battleships damaged the destroyers *Newcomb* and *Leutze* beyond repair. Ships on anti-submarine patrol in the middle ground between the pickets and the inshore forces were also repeatedly attacked, the destroyers *Hyman*, *Mullany* and *Morris* being severely damaged (the last beyond repair) as was the DE *Witter*.

The lack of tactical sense on the part of the inexperienced JNAF pilots, who were lured by the nearest ship and persisted in attacking destroyers which were plainly badly damaged and dead in the water, had deprived the Japanese of any chance of the local victory which was winnable on this day. The US troops ashore on Okinawa were beginning to run into stiffer resistance and the loss of the cargoes in the numerous transports and LSTs which were not found, or were ignored or missed by the suicide aircraft, would have had serious consequences. Even after the day's losses and casualties (including 363 men killed), the US Navy still had over 100 serviceable destroyers and destroyer escorts in the Okinawa area and half as many more with Task Force 58.

The 7th of April was the second day of the first *Kikusui* operation, but it is usually remembered as the day on which the Imperial Japanese Navy's surface fleet made its final suicide sortie, the battleship *Yamato* and most of her escorts being sacrificed to draw the US fast carriers into a *kamikaze* trap. The trap succeeded to a limited extent, for the *Hancock* was badly damaged by a lone *kamikaze* which set her hangar and aircraft

BELOW: 6 April 1945: Picket Station 1 at 1700 – the *Colhoun* accelerates away from the burning *Bush* (all but obscured by her smoke) as the station comes under renewed attack; 17 minutes after this photo was taken by the CAP, the *Colhoun* was mortally damaged.

RIGHT: 7 April 1945: noon – a destroyer on the screen shoots down a JAAF 'Nick' as TG 58.3 comes under suicide attack.

BELOW RIGHT: 1212, 7 April 1945: a suicide aircraft dropped a small bomb on *Hancock*'s forward flight deck.

on deck ablaze. Earlier, the destroyer *Bennett*, which had taken over on the exposed Picket Station 1, was severely damaged, as was the DE *Wesson*, on patrol near Ie Shima. The biggest raid to get through started out with 20 suicide aircraft, which were reduced to 14 by the CAP and then eight by the Kerama AA gun defenses – the eight survivors all missed their targets. In the last attack of what had been a relatively quiet day, the battleship *Maryland* was hit on the roof of her aftermost turret. The structural damage was slight, as were casualties, but she was withdrawn.

Only the picket destroyers were attacked on 8 and 9 April, one ship being put out of action on each day (*Gregory* and *Sterret*). Early on the 9th, the suicide boats enjoyed a rare success, badly damaging the anchored destroyer *Charles J Badger* and annoying the assault transport *Starr*, which was merely shaken. During the day, the defenses received a major reinforcement in the form of a Marine Air Group on Yontan airfield, within the Okinawa beachhead. Armed with 82 Corsairs and a detachment of Hellcat night-fighters, MAG-33 had the

dual role of close air support and fighter defense – under the current circumstances the latter became a priority.

After a day of bad weather on 10 April, Fifth Air Fleet made a determined attempt on the 11th to deal with Task Force 58, represented by just two groups (TGs 58.2 and .4). Thirty-six 'Zeroes' and 'Judies' began an hour-long raid in the afternoon by removing a radio antenna from the 'Tomcat' destroyer *Bullard* and then hitting her consort, the *Kidd*, flooding one of her boiler rooms. The CAP shot down a number of others from the wave, but a 'Judy' broke through and hit the *Enterprise* right aft, its 1100lb bomb exploding under the night carrier's stern. An hour later, another 'Judy' near-missed under her bow and the heavy underwater damage caused by the two explosions forced her to retire. The battleship *Missouri* shrugged off a direct hit on the armored belt and the *Essex* was superficially damaged by a near miss, as were two screening destroyers. Night attacks were completely unsuccessful, fighters and AA gunners adding 18 more victories to their daylight tally of 27. Ugaki had thus thrown away over 50 of his more skilled *kamikazes* against the hardest of targets.

They might have been better employed on 12 April, when *Kikusui 2* was launched. One hundred and eighty-five suicide aircraft (one third of them JAAF), and 45 torpedo-bombers were scheduled for missions, as were nine 'Ohkas'; 150 escort fighters would be available. As had happened six days pre-

viously, the *kamikazes* produced their 'big show' during the afternoon and again devoted disproportionate effort to Picket Station 1. The first raid of the series was a 30-'Val' strike which, despite losses to CAP and AA, managed to damage the *Cassin Young*, at 1346, but missed the *Purdy* and four LCS(L)s in company. Two ships from Station 2, to the east, were ordered to replace the damaged destroyer. A large raid appeared an hour later. From what happened during the next 15 minutes, this may have been a deliberate attempt to blind the

BELOW: Two Landing Craft (Support) motor across the bows of a Fletcher-class destroyer off the Okinawa beaches; on the evening of 22 April, *LCS.15* (left) was sunk outright by a *kamikaze*.

LEFT: *LST.829* at Kerama Retto – the panels on her sides are not anti-*kamikaze* armor but sections of floating causeway.

BELOW: The battleship *Idaho* firing against Japanese defensive positions on Okinawa; on 12 April the bomb carried by a near-miss 'Kate' caused minor flooding which ruined the beer stocks.

long-range defenses by knocking out the three most northerly picket stations (1, 2 and 14), for all came under coordinated attack almost simultaneously.

At 1445, the destroyer *Mannert L Abele*, on Station 14, was hit and her back broken by a 'Zero,' one of 20 which had approached. Not all these aircraft pressed their attack but they diverted the station CAP. A minute after the 'Zero' had struck, the *Abele* sighted a trail of smoke against the haze, just 1000 yards away – less than four seconds later she was hit in the forward boiler room by the first 'Ohka' to be launched in action. The destroyer's midships section disintegrated and she sank in less than three minutes, taking with her 79 men. Her supporting craft, *LSM(R).189* and *.190*, moved in to pick up survivors and themselves came under attack, *.189* taking a hit aft and *.190* being near-missed.

A minute after the 'Ohka' attack on *Abele*, the smaller *Stanly*, diverted from Station 2, became the second victim of the glider bomb. Her assailant dived through a dogfight between the CAP and *kamikaze* escorts but was diverted by AA fire which caused it to crash straight through the *Stanly*'s hull near the bows without exploding. The destroyer made for the repair base under cover of a CAP which protected her against further attacks, but not against a second 'Ohka' which carried away her ensign in overshooting into the sea. Station 1 held out until 1500, when the *Purdy* and two of the LCS(L)s – *.33* and *.57* – were hit by 'Vals,' three of which knocked out, but did not sink, *LCS(L).57. LCS.33*'s pumps were unable to cope with her flooding and she had to be abandoned. Station 12, to the west, saw only one Japanese aircraft – an 'Ohka' which hit the sea only 50 yards from the startled crew of the destroyer *Jeffers*.

Behind the picket screen, four DEs were attacked and the *Rall* and *Whitehurst* severely damaged. Off Kerama, the destroyer-minelayer *Lindsey* lost 60 feet (18m) of her forward hull when hit by a pair of 'Vals.' At the same time, 1450, the battleship group came under attack off Okinawa:

the *Tennessee* was moderately damaged by a 'Val' and the *Idaho* was near-missed by a Mitsubishi 'Kate' immediately after another 'Kate' had unwittingly created a thick smokescreen by wrecking the destroyer *Zellars*' forward superstructure. In the same general area, a minesweeper was slightly damaged by a near-miss 'Val.'

As off Mindoro, it must be doubted whether all the aircraft identified as Aichi 'Vals' were in fact the obsolescent navy dive-bomber; the army's Mitsubishi 'Sonia' and Nakajima 'Nate' also had fixed, 'trousered' landing gear and the *Rall* had been damaged by one of the latter. Whatever the type of aircraft, and the service flying it, it had again achieved less than the optimum performance. The destruction of Picket Station 1 was a temporary success which was not properly exploited, destroyers were still replaceable and battleships were practically impervious to suicide attack by aeroplanes. The glider bombs, though impressive, had been wasted on destroyers – it was not as though the pilots would learn from their brief combat experience.

As *Kikusui 2* started, there occurred the death of President Franklin D Roosevelt, only three months into his third term of office. The US Navy, which had lost 269 men in the 16 ships sunk and damaged on 12 April, at last broke to the public one of its best-kept secrets, the existence of *kamikazes*. Propaganda played down what effectiveness suicide attack had. The pilots were portrayed either as unwilling conscripts volunteered for death or as saki-crazed fanatics. As a gesture of contempt, the 'Ohka' was codenamed 'Baka' (fool).

A day too late, the Japanese Army on Okinawa launched a powerful counteroffensive on 13 April. No major suicide attacks developed and American troops enjoyed the aid of the warships' gunfire and the undivided attention of the US Marine Corps Corsairs and the escort carriers' Avengers, backed up by Task Force 58 dive-bombers. The Japanese ground attack was held and just one *kamikaze* got through to near-miss a destroyer escort.

The US fast carriers' 'Tomcat' pickets were attacked on 14 April by about 15 aircraft. The *Dashiell* was near-missed by three of them, another passed between the *Hunt*'s funnels, but the *Sigsbee* received a direct hit which snapped her port propeller shaft and she had to be towed back to Guam. Twenty-four hours later, during the afternoon of 15 April, Task Force 58 struck back, a fighter sweep catching Fifth Air Fleet by surprise to destroy 29 aircraft in the air and another 51 on the ground.

The sweep was timely, for it reduced the force available for *Kikusui 3*, which was launched in the early hours of 16 April, to just 120 JNAF and 45 JAAF suicide aircraft and a similar number of conventional bombers and decoys. By now the US Navy recognized the pattern of Japanese behavior before a 'big show': reconnaissance aircraft and 'snoopers' would appear in much greater numbers during the two hours before dawn, and single aircraft or small formations would appear at all heights to waste the CAPs' time in fruitless chases. Such activity to the north of Okinawa alerted the fast carriers on 16 April and a sufficiently strong CAP was held back to intercept the main raid when it appeared in the dawn twilight. This proved to be a group of 20 *kamikazes*, including a number of 'Bet-

BELOW: 'Ohka' glider-bombs were deployed to Okinawa before the US invasion but no use could be made of them as the airfields were completely neutralised by carrier aircraft; these provided their captors with an early opportunity to examine the weapon.

ties' carrying 'Ohkas,' escorted by a score of fighters. The US fighters destroyed all the attack aircraft and most of the escort long before they approached any Allied ship.

Strong CAPs were provided for the Okinawa radar pickets and the Marines over Station 1 fought valiantly against large numbers and at least 17 were shot down by the Corsairs but 25 others – 'Judies,' 'Vals,' 'Zeroes' and 'Oscars' – got through to attack the destroyer *Laffey* and *LCS.51* and *.116* between 0830 and 0940. Twenty of these attacked the destroyer and obtained five direct hits (all aft of the funnels) and three near misses. All power gone, on fire, with serious flooding and with 31 of her crew dead, she survived to be towed back to Kerama in a near-sinking condition. Both of the LCSs were damaged by direct hits. The destroyer *Bryant*, hastening to assist Station 1, was attacked by six more *kamikazes*, one of which damaged her severely by diving into the back of her bridge.

Only three 'Vals' were in a raid that surprised Station 14 at 0910. One missed *LSM(R).191* but the other two scored hits amidships on the destroyer *Pringle* and DMS *Hobson*. The forward engine room of the DMS was destroyed by fire, but she managed to reach Kerama under her own power; the larger *Pringle* was less fortunate, for the aircraft's bomb either blew up her boilers or detonated the forward torpedoes in their tubes – the explosion broke her in half and she sank in less than five minutes, with the loss of 65 men. This station, too, lost a reinforcing ship before it could arrive to give help – the DMS *Harding*'s near miss

The Japanese air forces, after expending over 800 suicide aircraft since the beginning of April, were unable for six days to muster enough aircraft for even medium-scale attacks. A few aircraft still approached and managed to get through, but between 17 and 22 April, the only ships damaged were an LSM and a minesweeper. Meanwhile, the troops ashore progressed well against grim Japanese resistance, taking the island of Ie Shima and putting an end to organized resistance in the north of Okinawa by the 22nd. Radar stations were installed in both locations, improving the defensive fighter coverage.

Shortly before sunset on the 22nd, a large coordinated suicide raid appeared, aircraft from Kyushu and Formosa taking part. The US Marine fighters shot down 34 of the 54

ABOVE: 14 April 1945: the destroyer *Sigsbee* (left), severely damaged after a suicide attack, is towed out of action by the *Dashiell*.

exploded alongside, blowing a large hole in her side and twisting her keel through 45 degrees. The *Harding* reached Kerama unaided but had been damaged beyond repair.

Behind the picket screen, only three ships were hit but all were badly damaged: the DE *Bowers* off Ie Shima and, to the south of Kerama, the oiler *Taluga* and an escorting destroyer, *Wilson*, hit by *kamikazes* from Formosa.

Task Force 58 came under attack during the early afternoon. At least four *kamikazes* got through, near-missing the *Missouri* and, 'by the skin of her bows,' the carrier *Bunker Hill* and her sister-ship *Intrepid*. Seconds later, another hit abaft the *Intrepid*'s after elevator, the engine and bomb going through to the hangar where the latter exploded, causing serious damage and starting a fire which raged for an hour. Only 10 men were killed, but the carrier was out of action for the remainder of the war. Task Force 58, now down to six Essexes and five light carriers undamaged, was reorganized as a three-group force by the dissolution of TG 58.2.

claimed by the defenses and for the first time Picket Stations 1 and 14 escaped without even a near miss. A destroyer on Station 15 was scratched by one suicider, but another scored a direct hit and sank *LCS(L).15* and, out to the west, the *Wadsworth*, on Picket Station 10, picked up a few splinters from a near miss. About a dozen aircraft, their formations broken up, made attacks on ships within the picket screen, but only five inflicted casualties, sinking the minesweeper *Swallow* and badly damaging the destroyer *Isherwood*, which sustained 42 of the 60 fatalities.

Four days went by without any loss or damage and with little sign of Japanese air activity. The suicide boats persisted but with no success against the vigilant 'Flycatcher' patrols. One of the more successful ships involved in these patrols, the destroyer *Hutchins*, was eventually caught unawares shortly after midnight on 27 April and damaged beyond repair by a well-placed depth-charge which exploded under her after engine room.

Kikusui 4 began with very little warning

at dusk. Only 65 *kamikazes* and 50 JAAF suicide aircraft were available and of these 25 were estimated to have attacked between 2000 on the 27th and 0400 on the 28th. The Marine night-fighters scored several victories, but the deliberate radar-guided stalk was unsuited to anti-suicide defenses and three aircraft got through to sink a Liberty ship, the *Canada Victory* (in spite of a smokescreen over the transport anchorage), damage the old APD *Rathburne* beyond repair and put out of action the destroyer *Ralph Talbot* – the last had survived worse damage in August 1942 off Savo Island.

It was the turn of the pickets once again during daylight on 28 April. Station 1 was attacked on 10 occasions during the afternoon but escaped damage. The *Wadsworth*, now on Station 12, lost one of her boats but was otherwise undamaged by a near miss; on Station 14 the *Bennion*'s after funnel was clipped by a *kamikaze* which sprayed her with gasoline; and *LCI.580* (Station 10) survived a direct hit with minor damage. The destroyers *Daly* and *Twiggs* on Station 2 vectored a Marines Corsair CAP to break up a large raid at 1700, but 40 minutes later they were themselves attacked by at least a dozen 'Vals.' Neither was hit but five near misses on the *Daly* riddled her port side with splinters and the *Twiggs*' hull was buckled by an underwater bomb explosion. One raid got through to Kerama and a hit on the 'hospital transport' USS *Pinkney* killed 35 personnel.

The *Pinkney* was not marked as a Red Cross vessel and the Japanese pilot cannot be blamed for this attack, but this was not the case of the individual who, at 2040, circled the floodlit, properly-marked hospital ship *Comfort*, 50 miles outbound for Saipan, before crashing into her. The 30 dead included an entire operating theater team and six US Army nurses.

Kikusui 4 petered out during the afternoon of 29 April with a final attack by two dozen *kamikazes* on Task Group 58.4's 'Tomcat' screen. These damaged the *Haggard* beyond repair, flooding all her machinery spaces so that she had to be towed to Kerama, and left the *Hazelwood* with severe blast damage and a fire that burned for eight hours as she too was towed clear. Fifty-seven men were killed and 66 injured in the two destroyers.

The final successful suicide attack in April occurred in the early hours of the 30th when a lone *kamikaze* on the Kerama anchorage hit the minelayer *Terror*, serving as the minesweeping force's HQ ship. Casualties were particularly heavy, 48

sailors losing their lives and 173 being injured, most of which were bad burns cases.

This last hit brought the number of ships damaged by suicide attack during April to 115. To achieve this, over 1000 Japanese pilots had either taken off with the intention of diving into a ship or had made up their minds in flight to convert a conventional bombing or fighter escort sortie into a suicide attack. A sizeable proportion of the pilots never survived to see a ship but were cut down by the US Navy or Marine Corps fighters; many others fell to the prodigious volume of AA gunfire that even a single US destroyer could put up; some missed because they simply could not cope, due to inexperience. Those who did hit, or missed by a margin narrow enough to cause damage, had sunk 10 ships and damaged eight others beyond repair. Sixty-one ships were sufficiently damaged to require them

to withdraw for repairs, a few to Kerama Retto but the majority to Pearl Harbor or the USA. Thirty-six sustained slight or superficial damage and were able to carry on.

The month of May began quietly, thanks in part to poor weather, with no casualties on the first two days. The rain and low cloud cleared at noon on the 3rd and Fifth Air Fleet threw in *Kikusui 5* beginning at dusk. The casualties on this evening suggest that the first raids came from Formosa or the Sakishima airfields, for they fell on Picket Stations 9 and 10, 55 miles to the west of Kerama. Both came under attack from about 1820, after the last CAPs had departed, and the 30-or-so *kamikazes* took their time.

The first ship to be hit was the destroyer-minelayer *Aaron Ward*, on Station 10, at 1822, by a 'Val' which left its engine in her after superstructure and a 'Zero' whose bomb exploded in the after engine room. Twenty minutes later, about 20 *kamikazes*

BELOW AND BELOW RIGHT: 4 May 1945: two views of the *Sangamon* at Kerama Retto on the day after she was *kamikazed*, with both her elevators blown out by the force of the hangar bomb explosion.

RIGHT: 1010, 11 May 1945: *Bunker Hill*'s fires burned for five hours after she was hit off Okinawa by a 'Zero' and a 'Judy'; 660 of her crew were killed or injured and the ship saw no further action.

concentrated on her consort, the destroyer *Little*, and scored four direct hits within the space of 90 seconds, all in the same area abaft the after funnel. The structural damage was catastrophic and the *Little* broke in half and sank at 1855. There was a brief pause, until 1900, and then there was a rapid succession of unsuccessful attacks until, at 1910, the *Aaron Ward*, *LCS.25*, which was helping her to fight her fires, and *LSM(R).195*, which was providing AA gun-fire support, were all hit. The DM survived four hits between the funnels and after gun, but lost all power, the LCS survived with little damage and the LSM had to be abandoned after her load of 100 bombardment rockets exploded in the fire. Eighty-five men died and 156 were injured on Station 10 in less than an hour.

On Station 9, the destroyer *Macomb* had been hit on one of the after five-inch gun

mountings at 1830 but was only moderately damaged and, apart from the loss of the gun, was able to fight on. The *Bache* had been near-missed but was undamaged and she was sent off to support the battered *Aaron Ward* after the *Little* was hit. While on passage to Station 10, she was again attacked, at 1910, by a suicide aircraft which dived under her bows. The attacks had ceased by the time that she arrived and she was able to escort the *Aaron Ward* under tow to Kerama, where she joined the grow-ing number of derelicts awaiting scrapping.

The next day opened as badly as 3 May had ended and was to finish with even heavier casualties. Kyushu-based *kami-kazes* began attacking Station 1 at dawn but the ships avoided damage for over an hour. The Japanese were either luckier or more skillful against Station 12, for 20 minutes after attacks began there, three broke through the CAP and sank both the *Luce* and *LSM(R).190*; the destroyer sank at 0812, just four minutes after she had been hit near No 3 gun, and took with her 149 men.

Thirteen minutes later, Station 1's luck ran out. Two 'Zeroes' dived vertically into the destroyer *Morrison*, blowing up her after boiler and opening the engine room to the sea. A few minutes later, she was hit again. It is an indication of how badly stretched her Marines Corsair pilots were that these hits were scored by two out of seven old float biplanes – Kawanishi 'Alfs,' one of which actually landed and taxied up the des-troyer's wake before 'hopping' into her after turret, which blew up. The *Morrison* sank rapidly after this final hit, with even heavier losses than the *Luce*: 159 men were dead and missing and 103 of the survivors were wounded. Her companion, the *Ingraham*, had already been stopped dead in the water by three 'Zeroes,' two of which had caused flooding by very near misses and one had hit her side, its bomb exploding inside the ship. The *Ingraham* was taken in tow for Kerama covered by *LSM(R).194* but they had not got far before, at 0850, another *kamikaze* hit the LSM, which sank rapidly.

Elsewhere, the destroyer-minelayer *Shea*, on Station 14, did not see an 'Ohka' until just before it hit her bridge structure at 585mph (936km/h). The warhead did not explode on impact and the fuselage tore straight through the bridge, killing 27 men, and exploded in the sea; the DM returned unaided to Kerama. Station 2 came under heavy and prolonged attack but the only hit, on the destroyer *Lowry*, bounced into the sea; she and her sister-ship *Massey* suffered only minor splinter damage.

The suicide attacks were aided by a thick

haze which made them difficult to spot by the fighters and AA guns crews, due to the aircraft's camouflage. The ships, on the other hand, were leaving highly-visible wakes as they maneuvered at high speed. About a dozen *kamikazes* broke through the picket screen and CAPs and came upon a group of minesweepers to the north of Kerama. The DMS *Hopkins* was slightly damaged, as were the motor-minesweepers *YMS.327* and *.331* and the fleet sweeper *Gayety*, the last despite being hit by a 'Zero' *and* an 'Ohka' – one of the few instances of a truly coordinated attack by aircraft and the glider bomb. While the attention of the CAP was distracted by this raid, a lone JAAF 'Oscar' flew low over Okinawa, avoiding radar detection and then pulled up to dive on the cruiser *Birmingham* at 0841. The engine went through two decks and the bomb exploded deep in the hull, causing extensive flooding and fires which burned for half an hour; another 51 men died and the ship had to withdraw.

In the space of just 50 minutes, 20 successful suicide pilots had sunk four ships and damaged eight others. Personnel losses were heavy, for 420 men had been killed or were missing and 470 more had been wounded or burned. The Japanese on Okinawa had mounted fierce counterattacks to coincide with *Kikusui 5*, but they inflicted fewer losses on the US troops than the JAAF and JNAF had done at sea.

The day was far from done. Small numbers of aircraft approached Okinawa but were held off until evening. To the southwest, off the Sakishima Gunto, the British carriers came under attack from Formosa. Hitherto, the British air defense organization had coped well with the *kamikazes*, holding them off well out of sight of the ships, but shortly before noon on the 4th, a single 'Zero,' undetected by radar, dived on the carrier *Formidable*, scoring a direct hit on the armored deck. The deck was merely dented, but by a freak event a scab off the back of the armor went straight down and punctured the ship's center boiler, reducing her speed to 18 knots; a dozen of her aircraft were destroyed and eight men were killed. Three minutes later, another 'Zero' evaded the 'Jack' patrol and slid off the *Indomitable*'s deck into the sea, causing no damage or casualties. Attacks continued for another hour, but only one more *kamikaze* got through, to near-miss the *Indomitable*, and the fighters and AA guns dealt with the rest.

The damage which a suicide hit could inflict on an unarmored carrier was well illustrated that evening. The veteran escort carrier *Sangamon* was operating to the west of Kerama when she was hit by a single-engined aircraft whose bomb went through her wooden flight deck and exploded in the hangar, starting serious fires, while blast caused severe splinter damage and both the elevators were 'dished' upward. Forty-six men were killed and 116 injured and the carrier was damaged beyond repair (she was, however, rebuilt as an oiler – her function until converted in 1942).

The last raid of the day took place at dusk with an attack on Station 10. The destroyer-minelayer *Gwin* lost a close-range AA control director to a hit and the destroyer

BOTTOM: 3 May 1945: 6 *kamikazes* hit the destroyer minelayer *Aaron Ward* within an hour on the evening of 3 May.

BELOW: 1100, 4 May 1945: a 'Zero' crashes into the water off HMS *Indomitable*'s port bow after bouncing off the carrier's armored deck.

Cowell picked up splinters from a near miss; but neither had to withdraw.

One hundred and twenty-five Kyushu-based suicide aircraft and as many as 60 *kamikazes* from Formosa had been employed during the 24 hours from dusk on 3 May and of these about one in five had delivered a successful attack. These had cost the US Navy three destroyers and three LSM(R)s sunk, damaged an escort carrier and a destroyer-minelayer beyond repair, and put a cruiser and three destroyers out of action. By contrast, the conventional attack aircraft which had also taken part had no success at all. *Kikusui 5* was by far the most successful mass offensive of the entire series but was a hollow victory. The Japanese Army's counterattacks, on the 33rd day of fighting on Okinawa, broke down with heavy loss in the face of American defenses, which enjoyed the massive support of naval gunfire which was little diminished by the withdrawal of the *Birmingham*, the only gun-line ship to be hit, and that, significantly, by a Japanese Army pilot. This small success merely underlined the poverty of the JNAF attitude. The navy had, to all intents, already given up any ambition of saving Okinawa and was devoted entirely to inflicting shipping casualties, regardless of value. The of 4th

May proved to be a turning point, for the American troops, who had been held in southern Okinawa, started to make minor gains at last, as the weakened Japanese began to give ground.

Two auxiliaries were slightly damaged in a pre-dawn raid on Kerama on 6 May and a small dusk attack was beaten off without loss on the same day. The war in Europe ended on 8 May 1945, but on the afternoon of the next day two of the Royal Navy carriers which had seen extensive hard service in that theater were hit by *kamikazes* from Formosa: the *Victorious* took two hits and the *Formidable* one, but suffered little material damage and, by US Navy standards, light casualties, while the 34 Corsairs which were written off were readily replaced. The battleship HMS *Howe* was near-missed. Two US destroyer escorts, the *Oberrender* and *England*, were damaged beyond repair at dusk while on patrol, losing 43 men dead between them.

After dark on 10 May, the destroyer *Hugh W Hadley*, on Picket Station 15, had a lucky escape when hit by an aircraft torpedo which failed to explode. *Kikusui 6* began the next morning and the same station took the first hits. The destroyer *Evans* was hit by four aircraft of the first wave and left on fire and dead in the water with her machinery flooded, to be towed to Kerama. The *Hugh W Hadley* was then singled out by 10 *kamikazes* which attacked her simultaneously from ahead and astern, followed immediately by an 'Ohka' – all either hit or were shot down. The piloted bomb exploded in the machinery spaces amidships and a bomb exploded in the after boiler room, flooding her to the main deck, while a crash on deck caused an extensive fire. Excellent damage control saved the ship but, like the *Evans*, she was fit only for scrap. *LCS(L).88*, one of three support craft on Station 15, was also hit and could not be repaired before the end of the war, now only three months away.

Another ship to be put out of action for the duration was the fast carrier *Bunker Hill*, Admiral Mitscher's flagship. Task Force 58 had been shadowed all night and fierce air battles had been fought beyond the 'Tomcat' screen, but no enemy aircraft had got within 50 miles of the carriers. At 1009, with only the briefest aural warning, a 'Zero' and a 'Judy' dived out of low cloud into the *Bunker Hill*. The fighter and its bomb set the after deck park alight and caused severe splinter damage, but the 'Judy' struck at the base of the island and its bomb exploded below the flight deck. The fires which swept the after part of the ship and the island were

BELOW: 1130, 4 May 1945: her center boiler-room damaged, the British carrier *Formidable* makes dense smoke; the anti-flash hoods and gloves issued to Royal Navy personnel minimised the number of burns casualties suffered in suicide attacks.

not subdued for over five hours and left 404 men dead, many by smoke asphyxiation, and 256 injured – the heaviest toll of any single attack. With 65 men killed on Station 15, this was also the highest single day's casualty bill for Operation Iceberg, even though no ship was sunk. The 150 suicide aircraft expended in *Kikusui 6* scored only two more hits on the 11th, on the destroyer-minelayer *Harry F Bauer* on Station 5, and on the Dutch merchant ship *Tjisadane* – the only ship of that nationality to be hit by a *kamikaze* – neither was seriously damaged.

Admiral Spruance's flagship, the battle-ship *New Mexico*, was the only casualty on 12 May. Two aircraft hit her at dusk, at the top and base of her funnel, causing splinter damage and fires. Fifty-four men were killed but the admiral, whose second experience this was, was again unhurt and remained on board as the ship stayed on station for another 16 days.

Thirty-five *kamikazes* attacked the Hagushi anchorage off Okinawa at dusk on 13 May. CAP and AA accounted for all but 10 of these, and the remainder made only two hits, severely damaging the destroyer *Bache* and the destroyer escort *Bright*. The former was particularly unfortunate, for her assailant was missing over the top of her until its wing tip clipped the mast, swinging the aircraft into her deck, where fragments and fire killed 41 men.

The Japanese record of success against flagships continued on 14 May. The fast car-riers had closed on Kyushu to attack 17 of Fifth Air Fleet's airfields, and although the US Navy strikes and sweeps were success-ful, destroying over 130 aircraft in the air and on the ground, Admiral Ugaki's *kamikazes* took advantage of their opportunity, even before their comrades began to suffer. The *Enterprise* had only rejoined Task Force 58 on 6 May after repairs to earlier *kamikaze* damage and Admiral Mitscher moved to her from the *Bunker Hill*. At 0700, the only 'sur-vivor' of a 24-strong raid got through the CAP and AA fire to hit the oft-damaged car-rier, destroying her forward elevator and causing a severe fire, but very light casual-ties. Again Mitscher transferred, this time to the *Randolph*, and again the *Enterprise* withdrew, this time for the duration.

Task Force 58's offensive success gave the Okinawa area nearly a week's respite from suicide attack. Only at dusk on 17 May did a small raid develop, four *kamikazes* from Formosa scoring a hit on the *Douglas H Fox* on Station 9. The destroyer's casualties were light and she made her own way back to Kerama.

An evening air torpedo attack on the Oki-nawa anchorage on 18 May scored one hit, on *LST.808* which was beached. Forty-eight hours later, at dusk on the 20th, three dozen suicide aircraft attacked the transport anchorages west of Okinawa but, with one exception, concentrated on the screening warships. The APDs *Chase* and *Register* were hit, the former being damaged beyond repair, as was the destroyer *Thatcher*. The DMS *Butler* and the DE *John C Butler* were slightly damaged. The exception was *LST.808*, already aground and written off by the torpedo hit: the abandoned hulk was destroyed by suicide attack.

Bad weather set in and did not lift until after sunset on 23 May. The improvement allowed Task Force 58's aircraft to strike at Kyushu, where they concentrated on the naval airfield at Kanoya, the HQ of Fifth Air Fleet and the most important single *kami-kaze* base. Eighty-four Japanese aircraft were claimed on 24 May, some of these being 'Ohka'-armed 'Betties' dispersed in sandbagged revetments. US Army Air Force Republic P-47 Thunderbolt fighter-bombers operating from Ie Shima made their first offensive sweep against Kyushu during the same day.

BELOW: Crewmen of the destroyer *Morris* examine the damage to their ship off Kerama Retto, 26 June 1945.

ABOVE: The *kamikaze* which hit the *Halsey Powell* crashed completely through her stern. Officers and men of the ship contemplate their comparatively lucky escape.

Thanks to the work of the fast carriers on 24 May, only 65 *kamikazes* were available for *Kikusui 7* on 25 May, but the JAAF was able to muster 100 aircraft. A few *kamikazes* made a series of attacks around midnight against the pickets and patrols in the northwest sector. The fleet minesweeper *Spectacle* lost 29 men and was abandoned when she was hit and the old APD *Barry* was hit on the bridge – fires were so severe that it was impossible to take the usual precaution of flooding her magazines, but there was no loss of life (apart from that of the *kamikaze* pilot). Like the *Spectacle*, the *Barry* was damaged beyond repair but in her case the decision was taken to tow her out of Kerama to be anchored as a 'tethered goat' to attract suicide attack.

Low cloud and rain cloaked the main attack of the day which was delivered between 0835 and 0905 – eight ships were hit in this period, only one of them a picket. *LSM.135*, carrying the *Spectacle*'s survivors, lost 11 men and had to be beached on Ie Shima when she received a direct hit, but the APD *Roper*, the DMS *Butler* (which had survived two near misses five days previously) and the destroyer escort *O'Neill* suffered no fatalities when they were hit and badly damaged, the first two ships beyond repair, in simultaneous attacks at 0840 off the west coast of Okinawa. Three more ships, two destroyers (*Cowell* and *Guest*)

and a destroyer escort (*William C Cole*), were superficially damaged by near misses in the same area. On Picket Station 15, the destroyer *Stormes* was hit by a *kamikaze* whose bomb flooded her after five-inch magazine and caused her weakened hull to sag. She reached Kerama unaided but lost 21 men.

The only other casualty of the day was the APD *Bates*. The converted DE was hit off Ie Shima by two *kamikazes* which killed 21 of her sailors and set her on fire so severely that she had to be abandoned. The *Bates* was towed to Kerama but her flooding spread unchecked during the night and she capsized in the early hours of 26 May. Later on that day, a solitary suicide aircraft appeared out of the low cloud off the east coast of Okinawa and wrecked the submarine chaser *PC.1603* with a direct hit which failed to sink the 280-ton craft.

Having lost nearly 200 suicide aircraft and escorts on 25 May, Fifth Air Fleet rallied quickly to begin *Kikusui 8* on 27 May. The weather was even worse, if anything, and was seriously interfering with US land-based air operations from Okinawa and Ie Shima. The USAAF P-47 CAP over Station 5, to the east of Okinawa, was recalled to base and soon afterward, at 0745, a small formation of 'Vals' attacked the destroyers *Braine* and *Anthony*. The latter escaped damage when near-missed, but two *kamikazes* hit

75

the *Braine* fore and aft of the bridge, setting her on fire and causing the evacuation of her machinery rooms; the *Anthony* towed her, still on fire, toward Kerama until a fleet tug could arrive. Sixty-six men were lost.

In mid-morning, time ran out for the DMS *Forrest*, which had been in the Okinawa area continuously for 64 days. She was hit and damaged beyond repair off Ie Shima with the loss of only five of her crew. There was then a lull until after dark, when a suicide raid reached the inshore areas and scored hits on three more ships, severely damaging the APDs *Rednour* and *Loy* (which lost six men between them) and *LCS(L).119*, 12 of whose men were killed.

The Okinawa defenses claimed only 47 Japanese aircraft shot down or destroyed by suicide on 27 May – fewer than half of the 110 JNAF and JAAF aircraft allocated to *Kikusui 8*. The offensive was resumed at dawn on the next day, when Picket Station 15 came under determined attack by twin-engined naval aircraft. Nakajima 'Irving' night-fighters and Yokosuka 'Frances' attack bombers were used, and the destroyer *Drexler* disintegrated and sank in 50 seconds when hit amidships by one of the latter. Over half – 158 – of her officers and men were lost with the ship and over 50 of the survivors were wounded. *LCS(L).52* was lucky to escape serious damage when she was near-missed by one of the big aircraft.

At 0940, a JAAF raid reached the main transport anchorage and inflicted the first damage on important resupply shipping for over a month, hitting five vessels. Unfortunately for the Japanese, only the merchant ship *Josiah Snelling* was at all seriously damaged, SS *Brown Victory* and *Mary Livermore* being barely scratched, while the assault transport USS *Sandoval* was able to continue unloading after a direct hit. The fifth ship to be hit was a small auxiliary, *YDG.10*, which also survived with little damage, however.

The final attack of *Kikusui 8* occurred shortly after midnight on 28/29 May. The *Shubrick*, on Station 16, about 30 miles northwest of Kerama, had been watching a 'snooper' for a quarter of an hour when it suddenly turned toward her and dived through AA fire to crash on the decking above the destroyer's after engine room. The big twin-engined aircraft tore a 30-foot (nine-meter) diameter hole in the deck and ripped out part of her side, causing heavy flooding. The water spread until, by 0130, her quarterdeck was awash and she was becoming unstable. The crew, less the 32 who had died, were taken off by a consort which stood by until the *Shubrick* was taken

in tow near dawn and brought to Kerama, where she was written off.

The Americans did not yet know it, but Fifth Air Fleet had virtually shot its bolt. *Kikusui 8* was the last large-scale suicide offensive. Ashore, the Japanese Army at last began to crack and the US Marines captured one of the principal defensive redoubts on 29 May. The next day was memorable for, for the first time in 66 days, no Japanese aircraft was detected in the Okinawa area, despite good weather. Admiral Halsey had relieved Spruance on 29 May and the fast carriers, once again designated Task Force 38, attacked Kyushu.

The weather closed in again on 2 June and the Japanese took advantage of this to begin *Kikusui 9*. This pale shadow of earlier offensives was spread over five days and involved only 50 aircraft – more had been dispatched as a single wave in earlier *Kikusui* operations. The absence of Task Force 38 on 4 and 5 June, when Halsey took the fast carriers and replenishment groups through yet another damaging typhoon, was an unexpected benefit to Fifth Air Fleet, but the results of the suicide attacks were poor, with *LCI(L).90* and the destroyer-minelayer *J William Ditter* damaged beyond repair, on 3 and 6 June respectively, and slight damage inflicted on five other ships, including the battleship *Mississippi* and the heavy cruiser *Louisville*, returned to duty after her damage off Lingayen.

Suicide attacks continued, with up to two dozen aircraft approaching on some days. Task Force 38 withdrew on 10 June to prepare for its next series of operations. Defense of shipping was undertaken by the shore-based fighters, supplemented by a reduced number of escort carriers until 24 June, when they, too, withdrew. The Corsairs, Wildcats and P-47s, with Hellcats by night, destroyed or turned back most raids during daylight and by night, but the difficulty of coping with dawn and dusk attacks remained, the Japanese proving to be adept at exploiting the period of changeover. Despite the small numbers of aircraft involved, these attacks inflicted relatively severe loss.

The first victim was the destroyer *William B Porter*, which was surprised on Station 15 by a single 'Val' an hour after dawn on 10 June. The aircraft missed but its bomb exploded under the ship and the shock opened welded seams under her machinery. The spaces quickly flooded and, without power to check the ingress of water, the ship foundered three hours later, without loss of life. Thirty-six hours later, at dusk on the 11th, Station 15 came under attack by three

ABOVE: 0700, 14 May 1945: a 'Zero', out of control with its port tailplane shot away, overshoots *Essex* to crash in the sea.

RIGHT: The destroyer/ minelayer *Lindsey* seen on 14 April 1945, two days after the *kamikaze* attack which caused the damage shown.

south coast of Okinawa on 18 June and three days later, at 1305, after 81 days of fighting, the island was declared secure. Fifth Air Fleet had not got the message and that evening launched the tenth and final *Kikusui*, to which 30 *kamikazes* and 15 army suicide aircraft were allocated. The JAAF appears to have been first on the scene, reaching the Kerama area from 1830. Five ships were hit or near-missed. The seaplane tender *Kenneth Whiting* was struck by fragments from a burning 'Oscar' which did little damage, and the *Curtiss* by a 'Frank' which scored a direct hit, killing 41 of her crew and starting fires which gutted half of the ship over the next 15 hours. The DE *Halloran* suffered minor damage from a near miss. The damaged APD *Barry* fulfilled her 'bait' role to perfection but she was actually being towed out to her decoy anchorage by *LSM.59* when both vessels came under attack and were sunk by hits off Kerama.

Kikusui 10 came to an end during the early forenoon of 22 June. An estimated 40 suicide aircraft and escorts were driven off Station 15 by Marine Corps fighters, which claimed to have shot down 29 aircraft. Some of the survivors diverted to the southeast coast of Okinawa, where *LSM.213* was hit but survived and DMS *Ellyson* was near-missed. At 0920, an enterprising Japanese pilot found *LST.534* beached and flew in through her open bow doors to damage her very badly and kill three men. It was the last attack of the Okinawa campaign, the last of over 1900 suicide missions. By 3 July, the defense organization was able to reduce the number of occupied picket stations to just two, 15 and 9A, covering the northeast and southwest approaches to Kerama.

Task Force 38 left Ulithi for what was intended to be the last series of attrition strikes on Japan before the invasion of Kyushu. Eight Essex-class and six light carriers began flying on 10 July with attacks on airfields and soon discovered that the Japanese had changed their strategy. No fighters took off to challenge the raids, the fleet was shadowed but not attacked and few aircraft of any type were found on the ground. The enemy, having been profligate with pilots and aircraft during the past months, was now hoarding them to repel the inevitable invasion. The fast carrier aircraft, to which the Royal Navy's contribution of four carriers, as well as two fresh Essex-class ships, was added from 18 July, were thus able to range freely over Japan, destroying the remaining major surface units of the Imperial Japanese Navy, much of the coastal shipping upon which inter-island traffic depended, the rail communica-

'Vals,' and *LCS(L).122* lost 11 men and was severely damaged by a hit on her bridge.

Five days later, on 16 June, during a small torpedo attack on shipping off the west coast of Okinawa, a 'Jill' 'fished' the *Twiggs* and, not content with the explosion of the destroyer's forward magazine, followed through by crashing into her after super-structure. Ablaze from end to end, the *Twiggs* sank an hour later with 152 of her crew.

The 1st Marine Division reached the

tions system and many industrial targets, opposed only by intense and accurate AA gunfire of all calibers.

The Royal Navy had its second experience of JAAF suicide attack on 29 July. A small task force was covering minesweeping operations off Phuket Island, with CAP supplied by two escort carriers. Warning was obtained of an inbound raid, but the Hellcats, never at their best at sea-level and burdened with rocket-rails, were unable to intercept before half a dozen 'Sonias' reached the separate groups. One aircraft was shot down as it dived on the carrier HMS *Ameer*, but a second hit the fleet minesweeper *Vestal*, setting her on fire so badly that she had to be abandoned and scuttled, losing 20 men. A third, pursued by a Hellcat, attacked the cruiser *Sussex*, which was itself bombarding Japanese positions, from seaward. Unfortunately, the available crew of the ship was much reduced by illness and insufficient men were available to crew the AA guns on that side. The 'Sonia' hit square on the hull, but did not penetrate the plating and left the imprints of its engine and fixed landing-gear on the ship's side.

A handful of attacks on the Okinawa area were attempted by suicide aircraft, probably from Formosa and Sakashima, at the end of July. Shortly after midnight on the 29th, a pair of 'Alf' floatplanes struck at Picket Station 9A. One near-missed the destroyer *Pritchett* but the other hit the *Callaghan* on No 3 turret causing an explosion. This was the destroyer's thirteenth and last experience of suicide attack. Her crew were unable to extinguish the fires or check the flooding and she sank two hours later with 47 of her people. She was the 28th and last destroyer and the 49th ship to be sunk by suicide attack. Another 'Alf' flew into the destroyer *Cassin Young* on Station 9A in the small hours of 30 July, severely damaging her, and another attack that night damaged APD *Horace A Bass* off southwest Okinawa.

The atomic bombs were dropped on 6 and 9 August, on Hiroshima and Nagasaki. On the second occasion, the fast carrier task forces (American and British) were off northern Honshu, where they had discovered a concentration of aircraft – 200 assorted bombers which were to have carried 2000 paratroop commandos for a *giretsu* attack on the Superfortress bases in the Marianas. That afternoon, the first *kamikaze* attack was delivered on the fleet for nearly three months. A 'Val' managed to reach the destroyer picket line undetected and dived into the rear of the *Borie*'s bridge, wrecking it, killing 48 men and starting fires which were controlled after two hours.

The *Borie* was not the last ship to be hit. That doubtful honor went to the assault transport USS *Lagrange*, which was hit in Buckner Bay, Okinawa, on 13 August in an attack which generally escaped notice outside the US Navy, so intent was the rest of the world on the larger issue of the impending end of the war.

There can be no doubt that the use of the atomic bomb prevented loss of Allied and Japanese life on a huge scale. Over three million Japanese were in arms on the Home Islands – Okinawa had had a garrison of under 80,000 but held out with little real support for over two months. Aircraft were still relatively plentiful, with 5300 available for suicide operations and as many again for conventional use. Five thousand pilots were under training, and though their experience would have been even less than that of the 2550 men who had died so far, they would be spared the long flights over water that their predecessors had faced during the Okinawa campaign.

But Japan now sued for peace and a ceasefire came into effect at 1100 on 15 August. This was an American initiative – the emperor did not order a ceasefire until the afternoon of the 16th. The delay gave some of those imbued with the spirit of *Bushido* a chance to die hard rather than live in defeat and they timed their last attack to coincide with the ceasefire. The Task Force 38 CAP, US Navy Corsairs controlled by HMS *Indefatigable*, obliged them by destroying most of the *kamikazes* which approached the Allied fleet – those that got through missed the ships. Vice-Admiral Ugaki, still in command of Fifth Air Fleet, chose to accompany this last attack and the legend grew that he had found death in flying into a warship. He did not – he died as vainly as all his brave young men had done, trying to turn back the clock by combining a primitive ritual with modern technology.

Ohnishi, the real originator of *kamikaze*, took his own life early on 16 August. His final message to the young people of Japan has, with nearly 50 years of hindsight, a curious ring: 'You are the treasure of the nation. With all the fervor of the special attackers, strive for the welfare of Japan and for peace throughout the world.'

It was estimated that 2550 suicide sorties had been flown. They either hit or near-missed close enough to damage ships on 363 occasions. Seventy-one of the ships were either sunk outright or damaged beyond repair, needing 110 individual hits; 150 attacks resulted in the ships requiring dockyard attention. Over 6600 Allied officers, men and women died.

ACKNOWLEDGMENTS

The author and publishers would like to thank Ron Callow for designing this book, Mandy Little for the picture research and Ron Watson for compiling the index. The following agencies and individuals provided photographic material:

Crown Copyright, pages: 72(top), 73.
Hulton-Deutsch Collection, pages: 53/Bettman Archive 48, 51(top).
Robert Hunt Library, pages 9(top), 15(top), 16, 24, 26, 27(both), 30, 40, 42(bottom), 46, 51(bottom), 54, 57(top), 58(top), 62, 65(bottom).
Imperial War Museum, London, pages: 1, 45, 47(top), 55.
MARS, page: 21(bottom).
Peter Newark's Military Pictures, pages: 11(inset), 23(both), 44.
US Army Photograph, page: 50(top).
US National Archives, pages: 6, 8(bottom), 9(bottom), 18, 20(both), 21(top), 22, 25, 28, 29(top), 32(both), 34, 41, 56, 59, 66(top), 67, 71(bottom).
US Naval Institute, Annapolis, pages: 12, 14, 19, 35, 38, 47, 58, 75/James C. Fahey Collection, 52/Mrs Marc A Mitscher 50(bottom)/National Archives 4-5/Smithsonian Institute 10-11, 33/US Navy Photograph 2(bottom), 13, 29(bottom), 36, 57, 60, 63, 64, 65(top), 68, 72(bottom), 74.
US Navy Photographic Center, pages: 2(top), 37, 66(bottom), 70(top), 71(top).